Edgar Allan Poe
Visitor from the Night of Time

Other Books by Philip Van Doren Stern

THE PORTABLE POE
THE ANNOTATED *WALDEN*
HENRY DAVID THOREAU: *Writer and Rebel*

Edgar Allan Poe
Visitor from the Night of Time

by Philip Van Doren Stern

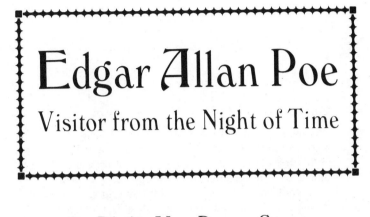
Thomas Y. Crowell Company · New York

Designed by Gai Moseley

Manufactured in the United States of America

Library of Congress Cataloging in Publication Data

Stern, Philip Van Doren.
Edgar Allan Poe, visitor from the night of time.

SUMMARY: Biography of an American writer who, in spite of his fame for such poems and stories as "The Raven," "Annabel Lee," "The Gold Bug," and "The Pit and the Pendulum," lived and died in poverty.

1. Poe, Edgar Allan, 1809–1849—Juvenile literature.
[1. Poe, Edgar Allan, 1809–1849. 2. Authors, American]
I. Title.
PS2631.S67   818'.03'09[B] [92]   72-83786

ISBN 0-690-25554-3
2 3 4 5 6 7 8 9 10

Contents

Edgar Allan Poe
Visitor from the Night of Time

1

The Early Years

Oh! That my young life were a lasting dream!
—"DREAMS," 1827

The year 1809 was a remarkable one, for a number of men who were to become world famous were born then. Among them were Abraham Lincoln, Oliver Wendell Holmes, Sr., Charles Darwin, Alfred Tennyson, William E. Gladstone, and Felix Mendelssohn. And Edgar Poe arrived in the world that year on January 19.

His paternal grandfather, David Poe, was a wheelwright and storekeeper of Irish descent who spent a fortune aiding the American Revolution. He got very little thanks and no reward except the courtesy title of "General" Poe. His son, also named David, abandoned his law studies to go on the stage. There he met a young actress, Elizabeth Arnold, and married her.

A son, whom they named William Henry, was born to

them in 1807. Since it was difficult for strolling players to take care of an infant, they placed him with his grandparents in Baltimore and went on to Richmond, and then to Boston, where Edgar was born two years later. This time they decided to try to bring up the child on the road.

The father was quarrelsome, difficult to get on with, and often drank too much. The unhappy couple remained together long enough for a daughter, whom they named Rosalie, to be born in 1810.

Mrs. Poe stayed on the stage and was acting in Richmond in the late autumn of 1811 when she became ill and died. Her husband is believed to have died about the same time.

Theater people in Richmond, Mr. and Mrs. Luke Usher, had taken care of the two children during the mother's illness, and they continued to do so for a few weeks after her death. Then, on the day after Christmas, a terrible fire destroyed the wooden structure that housed the Richmond Theater. The governor of Virginia and seventy-two others lost their lives there.

So many children were made orphans that day that the people of the city volunteered to take them into their homes. Although Edgar and Rosalie had not been affected by the fire, they too were given homes, Rosalie by Mr. and Mrs. William MacKenzie, and Edgar by Mr. and Mrs. John Allan.

The little boy was never formally adopted. The head of the household of which Edgar became a member was not one to take chances. John Allan had been born in Scotland only thirty-one years before, but he was already an old man, shrewd in business, strict in discipline, and as unemotional as one of the rocky crags of his native land. His wife, Frances, was very different. She was pretty, very feminine, and eager to mother the lonely little orphan. She spoiled him, people said, but he loved her for the affection she gave him.

When he was baptized a few weeks before his third birthday, he was given the name Edgar Allan Poe. Later, and with good reason, he abbreviated this to Edgar A. Poe, and that was how he nearly always signed his work and his letters.

John Allan was an exporter of tobacco, but he also ran a general store. Although he was well-to-do, his family lived in an apartment over the shop. His wife's sister stayed there with them, and she too is said to have spoiled the little boy.

Aside from the fact that he caught the usual childhood diseases like whooping cough and measles, very little is known about Edgar during these childhood years. At the age of five he was sent to what was then called a dame school, because it was taught by a woman rather than a man. Women were not considered in those days suitable instructors for boys and were allowed to teach only very young children, who required maternal care rather than formal lessons. In one of these early dame schools, Edgar was punished by having a vegetable of some kind hung around his neck and was sent home with it still dangling.

We know very little about Poe's school days, but we do know that he learned to read at an early age and was encouraged to show off this quickly acquired skill.

By every material standard, the child was well cared for. The family left Richmond in hot weather and spent the summers in the much cooler Blue Ridge Mountains. As a member of the Allan household, the young orphan was far better off than most children of his day. It seemed reasonable for him to believe that he would become John Allan's heir and live in comfortable circumstances all his life.

In the spring of 1815, Edgar was placed in a school taught by a man. But he was not allowed to stay there very long, for Allan, always the ambitious merchant, decided to go to England to set up a branch office there. He planned to stay for some years and take his family with him.

Even for ocean-going vessels, the James River was then navigable as far up as Richmond. Steamboats were still in the experimental stage, although John Stevens, John Fitch, Robert Fulton, and others had already built several of them. Because of the need for large quantities of fuel, the steam engine was regarded as impractical for long voyages. Yet the first Atlantic crossing by the historic *Savannah* was only four years away. But even that new ship was under sail most of the time; it used steam only as auxiliary power.

The Allans embarked on the sailing ship *Lothair* on June 22, 1815, and spent thirty-four days getting to Liverpool. This, and the return trip, were to be Poe's only ocean voyages. Yet he was often to write about the sea. He became much more familiar, however, with the passenger ships that connected the ports along the Atlantic Coast from South Carolina to Massachusetts.

From Liverpool, the Allans went to Scotland to visit relatives. They spent August and September doing this and did not arrive in London until October. Instead of going by sea, they traveled inland through Newcastle and Sheffield, and to do so they had to go by stagecoach, for passenger railroads were not yet in use. Journeying along the roads of England and stopping at the wayside inns for food and overnight stays gave them a good opportunity to see the countryside and visit a number of towns and cities. On the way, they passed castles, palaces, manor houses, half-timbered buildings, churches, and cathedrals. The 400-mile trip must have taken several weeks, for the coach was slow and made many stops.

Edgar Poe was seeing England at first hand. Young as he was, what he saw there made a strong impression on him, for most of his works have European rather than American backgrounds.

In London, the Allans found a place to live on Southampton Row, near the recently established British Museum. A few months after their arrival, Edgar was sent to a boarding school run by the Misses Dubourg on Sloane Street, halfway across London and far away from his foster parents. The Allans sometimes came to visit him and show him the sights of the city. The black ravens at the Tower of London made so great an impression on the young boy that he was never to forget them and would later immortalize a raven in his best-known poem.

In 1818, the Allans placed Edgar in the Reverend John Bransby's boarding school at Stoke Newington, which is now a part of north London, but which was then a separate village. It became the setting for his story "William Wilson," the most autobiographical of all his tales. Its hero even has Poe's own birth date.

In this story, Stoke Newington is "a misty-looking village of England, where a vast number of gigantic and gnarled trees, and . . . all the houses were excessively ancient." The school was in "a large, rambling Elizabethan house. . . . from each room to every other there were sure to be found three or four steps either in ascent or descent. Then the lateral branches were innumerable—inconceivable—and so returning in upon themselves that our most exact ideas in regard to the whole mansion were not very different from those with which we pondered upon infinity."

Poe spent two years, from age nine to eleven, in this strange old building. His best subjects were French and Latin, and he was introduced to the British way of life. The headmaster was a strict disciplinarian, but the school was not like the nightmarish one portrayed by Dickens in *Nicholas Nickleby*.

The schoolroom had "innumerable benches and desks, black, ancient, and time-worn, piled desperately with much-bethumbed books, and so beseamed with initial letters, names at full length, grotesque figures, and other multiplied efforts of the knife, as to have entirely lost what little of original form might have been their portion in days long departed. A huge bucket with water stood at one extremity of the room, and a clock of stupendous dimensions at the other."

Young as Poe was at Stoke Newington, he nevertheless began to write poetry there, and he wrote not only in English but in Latin as well. None of this verse has survived, but we know, from what he said later about it, that he was then very much under the influence of Byron. Poe was by nature a romantic, so it was only natural that so romantic a figure as the dashing, world-famous Byron should appeal to him. It took a number of years for him to escape from the Byronic influence, and even then, he was not able to free himself entirely from it.

The time spent in this British boarding school had an important effect on Poe. In Virginia he had already been taught to believe that aristocracy was the ideal form of government; his stay in England at an impressionable age confirmed this belief. At this time in his life, Poe had every reason to think that he would be a respected member of the ruling class, for he considered himself to be John Allan's heir.

Poe was in for a sudden shock, the first of many that were to come. In 1820, Allan's business in England was doing so badly that he decided to take his family home. The young Poe now saw how uncertain his luck could be. He also found out that a commercial trader like Allan could have his ups and downs, and that whatever fortune he might have was a long way short of the tremendous holdings of the European nobility the boy had been taught to admire.

His admiration for them is expressed in his writings, where nearly every character is rich, highly placed, and often has a title. In real life, Poe never met such people; they are part of his dream world.

On June 8, 1820, the Allans sailed on the *Martha* from Liverpool to New York and made the westward crossing in thirty-one days. Then they took a coastal ship to Norfolk and Richmond, and completed their journey on August 2.

Allan's quarters over his store had been rented out during their absence, so his family had to stay for a while with friends. Edgar entered Joseph Clarke's school, where he impressed its well-educated Irish owner with his knowledge of Latin,

French, and Greek. The time spent in England had improved his education. And it had also filled his mind with images of an older civilization, which he was to draw upon again and again in his work.

In Richmond, he continued to write poetry and addressed most of it to various young girls, sometimes making only slight changes from poem to poem. These also have been lost. Only one couplet of his earliest verse remains, and it, oddly enough, was written on a scrap of paper that John Allan had used for his commercial calculations. It shows that in November 1824, Allan had what was then the very large sum of $30,000 readily available for any need. The couplet, written in the precise and delicate script that makes all Poe manuscripts so attractive, reads:

—Poetry • by • Edgar A. Poe—
Last night, with many cares and toils oppress'd,
Weary, I laid me on a couch to rest—

Twenty-one years later, when Poe wrote "The Raven," he did it in clear handwriting that had changed very little over the years. The key word "weary" appears in both verses. So does the general melancholy effect.

Poe's interest in the dark side of life was beginning at an early age. So far, however, there seems to have been little reason for his addiction to morbid themes. With the Allans, he had always lived in great comfort, and Mrs. Allan acted like a fond mother to him. John Allan was another matter. Even while Poe was in England as a young child, he had found out how strict his foster father could be. But there he had been in boarding school. In Richmond he lived at home, where he was constantly under the eye of a man who believed that a growing boy needed a strong hand to keep him out of mischief. Allan was not cruel or malicious, but he had been brought up in Scotland, where discipline was the order of the day. Despite his $30,000 in assets, the income from his business was still small, so he vented some of his frustrations on the boy he had taken into his home.

At the age of fourteen, Poe had changed schools again and spent two years with another learned Irishman as his headmaster. He was still a healthy, athletic young lad who went shooting and skating. Like his hero Byron, he was at home in the water and once swam six or seven miles in the James River. He also took part in amateur theatrical performances, and in school excelled in reading Cassius' lines in Shakespeare's *Julius Caesar*. He liked to play practical jokes and at one time tried to frighten the elderly members of the Gentlemen's Whist Club by dressing up in a white sheet and a grotesque mask, pretending to be a ghost.

He now fell in love with the young mother of one of his friends, Jane Stith Craig Stanard. When she died early in 1824, he mourned her death and often used to go with her son to visit her grave. The death of a young and beautiful woman was to be a major theme in his work. One can see the origin of this obsession in his attachment to the unfortunate Mrs. Stanard.

His earliest full-length poem to be preserved, however, does not deal with women. It makes fun of a pretentious young Northerner named Bob Pitts, who was a clerk in a Richmond dry-goods store and who dressed with great splendor. The verses, entitled "Oh, Tempora! Oh, Mores!" show

little if any talent, but they cast some light on the way Poe
felt about his own uncertain position in Richmond society.
Pitts had made it evident that he thought he was too highly
placed to associate with the son of actors (then a despised
profession) who had no fortune of his own. Poe wrote this
poem to ridicule the young pretender and saw to it that copies
reached Jane Mackenzie's girls' school, where his sister Rosalie was a student. One evening, when he was asked to read the
verses aloud there, he was obviously so familiar with them
that he was charged with having written them. Since he did
not deny this, he was identified as their author. The jesting
lines identify the young clerk who had insulted Poe, and
townspeople quoted them in his presence, placing loud em-
phasis on his name:

> Because to his cat's eyes I hold a glass
> And let him see himself a proper ass.
> I think he'll take this likeness to himself.
> But if he won't *he shall*, the stupid elf,
> And lest the guessing throw the fool in fits,
> I close the portrait with the name of *Pitts*.

The satire had such an effect on Pitts that he eventually
left Richmond.

Poe would not seem the sort of person to be interested
in military life, but he was. Perhaps the colorful uniforms of
the time attracted him. He was only fifteen at this time, but it
was then the custom for very young men to get some training
in the militia. The Richmond Junior Volunteers was a group
that had social standing as well as glamorous-looking uniforms,

so Poe joined it and soon became a lieutenant. When Lafayette visited the city in October 1824, Poe served on the
honor guard that was appointed for the occasion.

On the surface, everything seemed to be going well, but
John Allan's attitude toward Poe was worsening steadily. On
November 1, he wrote to William Henry Poe, Edgar's older
brother in Baltimore, to say that Edgar was "sulky and ill-
tempered to all the Family. . . . The boy possesses not a Spark
of affection for us, not a particle of gratitude for all my care
and kindness to him . . . . I fear his associates have led him to
adopt a line of thinking and acting very contrary to what he
possessed when in England."

The fact that Allan's business was losing money soured
his rather dour disposition, but in March 1825 his uncle died
and left him more money than he had ever had. Overnight he
became a moderately rich man. He bought a fine house on
Main and Fifth streets, and his family, for the first time, had
a comfortable place to live in. Poe was given a room on the
second floor from which there was a view of the river.

Living across the street was a young girl, Sarah Elmira
Royster, with whom Poe promptly fell in love. According to
her, "he was a beautiful boy" but not very talkative. They
both took their mutual attachment very seriously and considered themselves engaged. But Mr. Royster did not approve.
They were both too young, he said.

They were not to be acquainted for very long, for John
Allan decided to send Poe to the University of Virginia in
Charlottesville. Off he went on February 14, 1826.

At the university, he was to specialize in Latin, Greek,
French, Italian, and Spanish. He had already shown that he

had a natural gift for language. He was just seventeen and could look forward to several years of study in subjects he liked and could do well in. But there was a self-defeating twist in his character. "The Imp of the Perverse," which he was later to describe in one of his stories, kept driving him toward destruction.

2

College and the Army

■✦✦✦■

Yes, tho' that long dream were of hopeless sorrow,
'T were better than the cold reality
Of waking life.

—"DREAMS," 1827

The University of Virginia was Thomas Jefferson's favorite project during the last years of his life. He designed the main buildings himself and intended this Charlottesville institution of higher learning to be a major influence in shaping American culture. He was still living in nearby Monticello when Poe arrived, but he was not to last out the year, for he died on July 4, the fiftieth anniversary of the Declaration of Independence.

Since Thomas Jefferson, who favored the formal Palladian style, liked to experiment with architecture and landscape gardening, the university he designed is both beautiful and unique. Nearly everything was built of the red brick that Virginia then excelled in, while the wooden trim was painted white. Separating the various sections are long, low walls also made of red brick. But they do not run in a straight line; they curve in and out and are therefore called serpentine walls. Jefferson said that they would last better than straight-line walls —and they have.

The university was very new when Poe arrived. It had officially opened only the previous year, and some of the buildings were not yet finished. But the one-storied West Passage, a long row of single rooms connected by a gallery, was ready, and Poe was assigned to Number 13. Since he could draw as well as write, he decorated its walls with pictures which he copied from an illustrated edition of Byron—and then added some caricatures of his professors.

The college day was easy enough, although it began at seven o'clock. Breakfast was served from eight to eight thirty; then there was another hour of classwork. But formal study ended at nine thirty, and the students had the rest of the day free. Nor were there any classes on Sunday.

The library was not ready until April 1826 and was open for only an hour a week until the end of October. Every possible obstacle to using books was placed in the way of the students. They had to apply in writing a day in advance for permission to enter the library, for books to be taken out, and even for consulting reference works. As was customary in college then, all the books were severely classical in content.

Poe applied only six times and then for works on history and language. He joined the Jefferson Debating Society and was considered to be a good speaker.

During the early spring of 1826, there was a violent disturbance in the college when an attempt was made to bring the "Hotel Keepers" under control. These were the men who were supposed to supply food to the dormitories, but they also encouraged drinking and gambling.

Poe described the disturbance in an early letter to Allan:

> The Grand Jury met and put the Students in a terrible fright—so much so that the lectures were unattended—and those whose names were upon the Sheriff's list—travelled off into the woods & mountains—taking their beds & provisions along with them—there were about 50 on the list—so you may suppose the College was very well thinn'd—this was the first day of the fright—the second day, "A proclamation" was issued by the faculty forbidding "any student under pain of a major punishment to leave his dormitory between the hours of 8 & 10 A M—(at which time the Sheriffs would be about) or in any way to resist the lawful authority of the Sheriffs"— This order however was very little attended to—as the fear of the Faculty could not counterbalance that of the Grand Jury— most of the "indicted" ran off a second time into the woods— and upon an examination the next morning by the Faculty —some were reprimanded—some suspended—and one expelled.

Poe was not involved in this, although he was summoned as a witness during the inquiry that followed. He then said that he had "never heard until now of any Hotel Keepers playing cards or drinking with students."

It is ironic that while the university's high-minded founder was still alive, it already had a student body that included many of the young Southern "bloods" to whom violence was a natural way of life. Fights were so common, Poe said, that no notice was taken of ordinary hand-to-hand combats. In one case, however, a young man struck another on the head with a stone, which prompted the injured student to draw a pistol and attempt to shoot his assailant, but the clumsy weapon missed fire. (Pistols, Poe remarked, "are all the fashion here.") A far bloodier encounter took place later that year when a ferocious young brute from Kentucky, having downed his adversary, deliberately began to bite his arm. Poe said that "it was bitten from the shoulder to the elbow—and it is likely that pieces of flesh as large as my hand will be obliged to be cut out."

It was disastrous for a person like Poe to be sent to a place where the worst elements of "Southern chivalry" were in command. Undoubtedly there were civilized and cultivated students among the 177 at the university, and Poe met a few of them, but he fell under the influence of the gambling, hard-drinking crowd.

He did not yet know how badly he was affected by alcohol, but he was soon to find out. He would drink a tumbler of peach brandy and quickly become so befuddled that he did not know what he was doing when he played cards with students who had long ago become used to consuming large amounts of alcohol and were experts at the gaming table. Naturally he lost—again and again. Poe blamed John Allan for his troubles. It was Allan, he said, who had brought him up to believe that he was a wealthy man's heir, able to rank socially and financially with the sons of great plantation owners. Now Allan refused to give him enough money even to pay his ordinary expenses. Something had happened to make the relationship between Poe and his foster father deteriorate still further.

John Allan had been having an affair with a woman with whom he had three illegitimate children. In a small town like

Richmond, Poe would surely have learned about this and very likely had words with Allan about it. The guilty and angry foster father would resent such interference in his private affairs and want to get rid of the outspoken boy. Sending him to Charlottesville was a solution. Then he naturally resented every cent he had to spend on him.

At the University of Virginia, where each student was supposed to have a manservant of his own, Poe now found himself so short of money that he was constantly embarrassed. He explained this later in a letter to Allan:

I will boldly say that it was wholly and entirely your own mistaken parsimony that caused all the difficulties in which I was involved while at Charlottesville. The expenses of the institution at the lowest estimate were $350 per annum. You sent me there with $110. Of this $50 were to be paid immediately for board—$60 for attendance upon 2 professors—and you even then did not miss the opportunity of abusing me because I did not attend 3. Then $15 more were to be paid for room-rent—remember that all this was to be paid in advance, with $110. $12 more for a bed—and $12 more for room furniture . . . . You will remember that in a week after my arrival, I wrote to you for some more money, and for books. You replied in terms of the utmost abuse—if I had been the vilest wretch on earth you could not have been more abusive than you were because I could not contrive to pay $150 with $110. I had enclosed to you . . . an account of the expences [sic] incurred amounting to $149—the balance to be paid was $39. You enclosed me $40, leaving me one dollar in pocket.

As a result, Poe had to borrow from professional money-lenders in Charlottesville who charged him an exorbitant rate of interest. It was then, he said, that he became dissolute, for he could not associate with any students except those who were in similar circumstances. "They," he added, "from drunkenness and extravagance." But in his case, he protested, "because it was my crime to have no one on Earth who cared for me, or loved me. I call God to witness that I have never loved dissipation. . . . But I was drawn into it by my companions."

He became desperate and gambled still more in a reckless attempt to regain his losses. Before the year was out, he had lost $2000—an enormous amount of money at a time when workingmen were paid 50 cents a day and a black human being could be bought outright for a few hundred dollars. It is entirely possible that the unprincipled and greedy young scoundrels, with whom he was playing on credit he did not have, took advantage of the innocent Poe, especially when alcohol was beclouding his reason and caution.

Poe made use of his experiences in his autobiographical story, "William Wilson." The scene was transferred to Eton and Oxford, and the transgressions were magnified into sins far worse than gambling or drinking. But readers of that story will note the resemblance to this period in Poe's own life.

When the term ended on December 15, 1826, Poe was cited for his excellence in Latin and French. But after ten months, his career at the University of Virginia was over, for John Allan refused to pay for another term.

Poe's life had many low spots in it, but this period was one of the worst. When he returned to Richmond, to stay again in John Allan's house, he found out that the love letters he had written to Elmira Royster had been intercepted by her father, who thought that his seventeen-year-old daughter was too young to receive such messages. But she was not too young to become engaged to marry Alexander B. Shelton while Poe was at the university. He must have been heart-broken, but at a time when everything is going wrong, one more disaster loses some of its impact.

Very little is known about him for the next few months. Then matters came to a head that spring. A letter, dated March 25, 1827, written to Poe by a friend named Edward G. Crump shows that the two had met recently, and that Poe owed Crump money which was not a gambling debt. This may have come to the attention of Allan—or perhaps something else caused the break. At any rate, on Monday, March 19, Poe wrote to Allan to say that he was determined to leave his house. Actually, he had already been ordered out. There had been a violent disagreement which led to angry words over an opinion (not described) that Poe had expressed. He asked that his trunk and enough money to pay for a ticket to Boston be sent to the Court House Tavern. He was not staying there, however, because he could not pay for a room.

Another letter, dated the next day, shows how serious his situation was. He had nowhere to sleep and had to roam the streets. And, he wrote: "I have not one cent in the world to provide any food."

It must have humiliated Poe to have to ask Allan again for the $12 he needed for passage on a ship to Boston. It is not known whether Allan sent him any money or not, but somehow—perhaps from Mrs. Allan—Poe got enough to en-able him to embark on a northbound vessel.

He did not go directly to Boston. Instead, he left the

ship at Norfolk and went from there to Baltimore, where he probably saw his older brother, William Henry, who also wanted to be a poet.

When Poe finally got to Boston, he may have been a merchant's clerk and then a market reporter for a short time. Whatever his work was, it could not have been to his liking, for on May 26, 1827, he enlisted in the Army under the name Edgar A. Perry. This was not the first or the last time he assumed false names. A note which Allan wrote on Edward Crump's letter of March 25 states that it was addressed "to E. A. Poe, alias Henri Le Rennet."

Poe's enlistment record gives us a precise physical description: "Height, five feet, eight inches; eyes, grey; hair, brown; and complexion, fair." It also says that he "was assigned to Battery H, 1st U. S. Artillery, then stationed at Fort Independence, Boston Harbor."

The new private was ashamed of his lowly rank, for later instead of admitting that he had served in the American Army, he said that he had been in St. Petersburg, Russia, and also that he had fought for Greek independence.

But the most important thing that occurred during Poe's army career had nothing to do with military affairs. He had a great deal of time on his hands, during which he read widely and wrote poetry. He had quite a batch of early poems ready now, enough to make a slim little book. He met Calvin Thomas, a young printer with a shop of his own, and persuaded him to publish a volume of his poetry, entitled *Tamerlane and Other Poems*. It was not signed, but the title page read: "By a Bostonian." Poe believed that the Boston public would be more receptive to one of its own people than to an outsider. And he had, of course, been born there, although he had not seen the city since he was an infant.

This slight deception was echoed in the short preface in which Poe said: "The greater part of the Poems were written in the year 1821-2, when the author had not completed his fourteenth year." During that year, he had been in Joseph Clarke's school in Richmond where he wrote some verses addressed to various young girls in that city and was busy studying Latin. He may, however, have gotten the idea for "Tamerlane" at this time. Christopher Marlowe, Nicholas Rowe, and the Gothic novelist Matthew Gregory ("Monk") Lewis had been inspired to write plays about this noted figure. Since Lewis' dramatic spectacle—complete with horses—had been staged three times in Richmond during the last half of 1822, Poe could have become interested in the Oriental conqueror's remarkable career then. His long poem, however, has almost nothing to do with the real Tamerlane (1336?-1405), who was born poor and remained illiterate all his life. He was lame from having been injured in a sheep-stealing raid during his youth. He rose rapidly as the leader of an invading army that created an empire for him which stretched from the Black Sea to India.

The Tamerlane in Poe's poem is a much gentler and kinder person than the fierce historical figure who was noted for the mass slaughter of prisoners. In Iran he built a monument to himself by piling up a heap of seventy thousand skulls.

The poem is supposedly spoken by Tamerlane just before his death, but it relates far more directly to Poe's rejected love for Elmira Royster than it does to anything connected with the far-distant ruler.

Several other poems in the book may also refer to Elmira, especially the ones beginning "I saw thee on thy bridal day," "In visions of the dark night I have dreamed of joy departed," and

> The happiest day—the happiest hour
> My sear'd and blighted heart hath known,
> The highest hope of pride, of power,
> I feel hath flown.

The last poem in the little book, "The Lake," is about a twilight visit to a desolate lake, perhaps in the Dismal Swamp near Norfolk, Virginia. It was originally a part of "Tamerlane," but Poe revised it several times and published it separately. It shows a surer hand at poetic composition than most of his early poems do:

> In youth's spring, it was my lot
> To haunt of the wide earth a spot
> The which I could not love the less;
> So lovely was the loneliness
> Of a wild lake, with black rock bound,
> And the tall trees that tower'd around.
> But when the night had thrown her pall
> Upon that spot—as upon all,
> And the wind would pass me by
> In its stilly melody,
> My infant spirit would awake
> To the terror of the lone lake.
> Yet that terror was not fright—
> But a tremulous delight,

And a feeling undefin'd,
Springing from a darken'd mind.
Death was in that poison'd wave
And in its gulf a fitting grave
For him who thence could solace bring
To his dark imagining;
Whose wild'ring thought could even make
An Eden of that dim lake.

With the publication of *Tamerlane and Other Poems*, Poe could consider himself a full-fledged poet. The edition was exceedingly small, the price low, and the sale negligible. As a result, this tiny book, hardly more than a pamphlet, has become one of the highest-priced printed rarities in American literature. Poe manuscripts, of course, are worth even more.

Tamerlane was not reviewed, and hardly anyone knew of its existence. Today poets are unhappy at the silence that usually greets their first book. But few volumes of poetry get off to a worse start than *Tamerlane* did.

3

In and Out of West Point

■✦✦✦■

*I have thrown myself on the world . . . I must
either conquer or die—succeed or be disgraced.*

—LETTER TO JOHN ALLAN, December 1, 1828

During the autumn of 1827, the battery in which Poe served
was transferred to Fort Moultrie on Sullivan's Island in
Charleston Harbor, South Carolina. He went by ship and
arrived at the fort on November 18. He was to remain there
for more than a year.

Sixteen years later, when he used the island as the setting
for his story, "The Gold-Bug," he described it:

> It consists of little else than the sea sand and is about
> three miles long. Its breadth at no point exceeds a quarter of
> a mile. It is separated from the main land by a scarcely per-
> ceptible creek, oozing its way through a wilderness of reeds
> and slime, a favorite resort of the marsh-hen. The vegetation,
> as might be supposed, is scant, or at least dwarfish. No trees
> of any magnitude are to be seen. Near the western extremity

where Fort Moultrie stands, and where are some miserable frame buildings, tenanted, during summer, by the fugitives from Charleston dust and fever, may be found, indeed, the bristly palmetto; but the whole island, with the exception of this western point, and a line of hard, white beach on the seacoast, is covered with a dense undergrowth of the sweet myrtle, so much prized by the horticulturists of England. The shrub here often attains the height of fifteen or twenty feet, and forms an almost impenetrable coppice, burthening the air with its fragrance.

Scenes from other stories—"Metzengerstein," "The Balloon Hoax," and "The Oblong Box"—also show that Poe had opportunities to explore the Charleston area and store its locations in his memory. He was made company clerk, and was then given certain minor privileges. He became friendly with his company commander, Colonel William Frayton, to whom he later dedicated *Tales of the Grotesque and Arabesque*.

Everyone in the company knew that Poe was an educated man, far different from the farm lads and city outcasts who enlisted in the Army then. It is hard to think of so undisciplined a person as Poe becoming a good soldier, but he always applied himself diligently to his work, whatever it was, and in performing it he was serious, attentive, and efficient.

His term of enlistment was for five years, and he now began to have some qualms about being deprived of a higher education. He explained his feelings to a sympathetic officer who promised to help him gain a discharge from the Army if he would write to John Allan and become reconciled with him. On December 1, when the unit was about to be sent to Fortress Monroe, Virginia, Poe overcame his pride and wrote a long letter to his foster father. He pointed out that the lengthy enlistment period would cause the prime of his life to be wasted and then added: "I am altered from what you knew me, and am no longer a boy tossing about on the world without aim or consistency."

The battery went on to Fortress Monroe, but no reply came from Allan. Poe tried to convince himself that perhaps his letter had not been received and sent a second one, practically repeating the first. Still no answer.

On January 1, 1829, Poe was made a sergeant major, the highest rank a noncommissioned soldier could then attain. This promotion, and the fact that he had had a year in college, put him in a good position to apply to West Point for a cadet's appointment. He asked John MacKenzie, who had adopted Poe's sister Rosalie, to intercede for him with Allan; he then wrote to Allan again to tell him about his chance for a free education at the United States Military Academy. His letter, dated February 4, 1829, closes with "Give my love to Ma." This was his last message to the only mother he had ever known, for Mrs. Allan died before the month ended.

Poe was given leave of absence to attend her funeral, but by the time he arrived in Richmond his foster mother was already in her grave. The occasion, however, brought about a temporary reconciliation with John Allan. During this brief visit, Allan was won over to the idea of helping him obtain an appointment to West Point, and Poe's next letter to him is addressed to "My dear Pa." In it he said that he was busy preparing himself for the tests that he would have to take for admission to the Military Academy.

Poe was to be permitted to leave the Army if he could

get someone to substitute for him. The normal bounty for this was $12, but Poe had to use $75 of the $100 Allan had just given him. For this fee he was able to induce a sergeant in his company to reenlist. He was then discharged on April 15 and left Fortress Monroe with several testimonials signed by higher officers there. He also got one from John Allan, which stressed the fact that Poe was the grandson of Quartermaster General David Poe, who had done so much for his country during the Revolution.

He evidently spent some time in Richmond and visited Washington early in May to present his application in person to the Secretary of War. He then went on to Baltimore, where he met his grandmother (the widow of the general); his brother, William Henry; his paternal aunt, Mrs. Maria Clemm; and her seven-year-old daughter, Virginia.

Poe was now waiting to hear from West Point. An appointment there would solve his most pressing problem—the daily one of having enough to eat, a place to sleep, and clothes to protect him from the cold. He stayed in Baltimore, still eager to get his work (which was all in verse at this time) published, so it would reach an audience and make his name known. He went to Philadelphia with a collection of poems for a book to be entitled *Al Aaraaf, Tamerlane, and Minor Poems* and delivered this with a long letter to Carey, Lea, and Carey, noted book publishers in that city.

He also wrote to John Allan, trying to persuade him to guarantee the publishers against loss (a sum not to exceed $100), and telling him that he had "long given up *Byron* as a model—for which, I think, I deserve some credit."

Byron had died in 1824, and by 1829 his fame was already beginning to fade. The fact that Poe believed that he had escaped from Byron's excessively romantic influence shows that he was becoming more mature. This, however, does not mean that he was to be less of a romantic. He was to be one all his life, but not of the Byronic kind.

Allan refused to give any assistance, and the publishers held on to the manuscript. Meanwhile Poe was robbed by a cousin of the little money he had. He wrote again to Allan but got no reply. Finally, late in July, Allan sent some money, and Poe went to Washington again to expedite his application to West Point. He made the journey, not by coach, but on foot both ways. He knew the value of money now and was trying to make it go as far as possible.

The appointments for September were announced, but Poe's name was not among them. This meant that he had to wait for the March list.

When he wrote to Allan again, he described the plight of his Baltimore relatives: "My grandmother [General Poe's widow] is extremely poor and ill (paralytic). My aunt Maria if possible still worse and Henry [William Henry, Poe's brother] entirely given up to drink and unable to help himself, much less me."

Poe asked Carey and Lea to return the manuscript of *Al Aaraaf* and managed to find someone else to issue it. The new publishers, Hatch and Dunning of Baltimore, were willing to compensate the author by giving him 250 copies of his 72-page book. When it appeared in December, he sent one to John Allan.

Al Aaraaf, like Purgatory, but Arabian in concept, is a place between Heaven and Hell that is supposed to be located in a star discovered by Tycho Brahe in 1572. For a brief time this star was brighter than Jupiter, but it soon faded and disappeared. There, according to Poe, "men suffer no punishment, but yet do not attain that tranquil or even happiness which they suppose to be characteristic of heavenly enjoyment." And Al Aaraaf has nothing in common with our world except beauty, which is rare here but not there. Keats, Thomas Moore, Milton, Chateaubriand, Byron, the Bible, and Oriental literature all had an influence on this long poem. In it the name Ligeia is used; it was to appear again in one of Poe's most famous short stories.

"Al Aaraaf" is Poe's longest poem and one of his most difficult, for he uses it as a vehicle to present his views about beauty, truth, poetry, God, and the nature of the universe. It is remarkable that a twenty-year-old private in the army should not only have such ideas but be able to express them well enough in verse to get them printed.

The poem covers many subjects and has many characters. One of them is Michelangelo, who is brought in as a creator of beauty:

> He was a goodly spirit—he who fell:
> A wanderer by mossy-mantled well—
> A gazer on the lights that shine above—
> A dreamer in the moonbeam by his love:
> What wonder? for each star is eye-like there,
> And looks so sweetly down on Beauty's hair—
> And they, and ev'ry mossy spring were holy
> To his love-haunted heart and melancholy.
> The night had found (to him a night of woe)
> Upon a mountain crag, young Angelo—

Beetling it bends athwart the solemn sky,
And scowls on starry worlds that down beneath it lie.
Here sate he with his love—his dark eye bent
With eagle gaze along the firmament:
Now turn'd it upon her—but ever then
It trembled to the orb of EARTH again.

The volume also contains a cut-down version of "Tamer-lane" and ten short poems. They are all written in the fervid, romantic vein that was then popular. More characteristic of Poe was a short poem which he wrote in a lady's autograph album at this time:

ALONE

From childhood's hour I have not been
As others were—I have not seen
As others saw—I could not bring
My passions from a common spring—
From the same source I have not taken
My sorrow—I could not awaken
My heart to joy at the same tone—
And all I loved—*I* loved alone—
Then—in my childhood, in the dawn
Of a most stormy life—was drawn
From every depth of good and ill
The mystery which binds me still—
From the torrent, or the fountain—
From the red cliff of the mountain—
From the sun that round me rolled
In its autumn tint of gold—
From the lightning in the sky
As it pass'd me flying by—

From the thunder, and the storm—
And the cloud that took the form
(When the rest of Heaven was blue
Of a demon in my view—)

The original had no title; the word "Alone" was placed on it by an editor many years later.

The publication of Al Aaraaf attracted little attention, but it did get two reviews, neither of which helped either its sale or Poe's reputation very much.

The Ladies Magazine said: "Parts are exceedingly boyish, feeble, and altogether deficient in the common characteristics of poetry; but then we have parts too of considerable length which remind us of no less a poet than Shelley. The author, who appears to be very young, is evidently a fine genius, but he wants judgment, experience, tact." The Baltimore Minerva was less kind. It called Al Aaraaf "a pile of brick bats" and dismissed Tamerlane by saying that "its faults are so few and so trifling that they may be passed over."

Poe evidently spent some time in John Allan's home during the early spring of 1830. His appointment to the Military Academy arrived in March; he was to report there late in June.

In May, his Army substitute wrote to him complaining that he had not received some money Poe had borrowed from him. In his reply, Poe said that he had not been able to get anything from Allan and then added that his foster father was "not very often sober." It was an unfortunate remark, for the substitute sent the letter to Allan.

But relations between them were already bad. Poe later

told Allan that he had written this letter "within a half hour after you had embittered every feeling of my heart against you by your abuse of my *family*, and myself, under your roof— and at a time when my heart was almost breaking."

Despite this, Poe stayed on in Richmond for several weeks and then left there on May 21. Oddly enough, John Allan accompanied him to the steamboat landing. When they parted, Poe felt that he would probably never see him again.

He stayed for some time in Baltimore, perhaps with Mrs. Clemm and Virginia, and then arrived at West Point late in June. There he had to take entrance examinations, which he passed, although he said that a number of applicants "of good family" failed. He also told Allan that "of 130 Cadets appointed every year only 30 or 35 ever graduate—the rest being dismissed for bad conduct or deficiency. The Regulations are rigid in the extreme."

West Point was a very strict place with military discipline ruling every moment of the student's life. The summer months were spent in an outdoor camp, and studies began in earnest in the fall when the cadets returned to the Academy, which consisted of a few barracks-like buildings facing an open parade ground. There were two barren-looking dormitories, a mess hall, a library, a chapel, and an ugly two-story edifice which provided space for classrooms. A few older buildings were left over from the Revolution. The location, however, had a fine view of the Hudson and the mountains.

Classes began at sunrise; breakfast was at seven; then there were more classes. Engineering studies dominated the curriculum. Military drill took place during the late afternoon. After dinner, there were still more classes. At ten o'clock lights were supposed to go off. Punishment for any infraction of the 304 regulations was swift and drastic. No books not connected with the studies were allowed. Neither were games of any kind. Drinking or smoking, of course, were strictly forbidden.

But some of the cadets defied the rules and were disciplined and often dismissed. It was a hard life, intentionally made so, for a man who wanted to be an officer had to learn to stand all sorts of difficulties and surmount them without being broken in spirit.

The records show that Poe was third in French and seventeenth in mathematics in a class of eighty-seven, so he was doing quite well scholastically. But he was bored by the endless drill, which he knew by heart from his experience in the Army. One of his classmates told his mother that "Mr. Poe . . . ran away from his adopted father in Virginia who was very rich, has been in S. America, England, and has graduated from one of the Colleges there." Poe was spinning romantic and fanciful tales about himself to bolster up his standing in the eyes of his fellow cadets. And he was drinking again.

When John Allan remarried on October 5, 1830, news of the wedding quickly reached Poe. He wrote to his foster father a month later but said nothing about the marriage except to offer his respects "to Mrs. A." among others. After this, his relations with the Allans rapidly worsened. The first Mrs. Allan had treated him like a mother; the second one hardly knew of his existence.

Examinations were held on January 3, 1831, and by this time Poe had had enough of West Point, military life, engineering, mathematics, and strict discipline. He had recently received a bitter letter from Allan, and he replied to it on that unhappy day. After summarizing the way Allan had treated him all his life, he said:

> You sent me to W. Point like a beggar. The same difficulties are threatening me as before [at the University of Virginia]— and I must resign . . . . It will be necessary that you (as my nominal guardian) enclose me your written permission. It will be useless to refuse me this last request—for I can leave the place without your permission—your refusal would only deprive me of the little pay which is now due as mileage. From the time of this writing I shall neglect my studies and duties at the institution—if I do not receive your answer in 10 days—I will leave the point without—for otherwise I should subject myself to dismission.

No reply came from Allan, and Poe deliberately cut classes, did not show up for roll call, and refrained from going to chapel, even after having been ordered to do so. On January 28 he was court-martialed and dismissed. He was allowed to stay until March 6, but he left on February 19 and went to New York City.

He used those last days at the Academy to circulate a subscription list among the cadets for a new book of poetry for which he had found a publisher in New York. The price to the cadets for the little volume was only 75 cents, but he cannot have sold many copies in so small an institution.

He went from West Point to New York without adequate clothing and caught a cold on the way. A serious ear infection developed, and he became so ill that he wrote in semidelirium to John Allan, again pleading for aid. As usual, he did not get an answer.

In the poem entitled "Introduction" are lines that sum

up Poe's attitude toward life and literature at the age of twenty-two:

> I fell in love with melancholy. . . .
> I could not love except where Death
> Was mingling his with Beauty's breath

This obsession with melancholy and the death of a beautiful woman was to run through much of Poe's work. Thirteen years later, he was still dominated by dreams and darkness. In "Dream-Land," which was first published in 1844, he wrote:

> By a route obscure and lonely,
> Haunted by ill angels only,
> Where an Eidolon, named Night,
> On a black throne reigns upright,
> I have reached these lands but newly
> From an ultimate dim Thule—
> From a wild weird clime that lieth, sublime,
> Out of Space—out of Time.

Poe had made arrangements with a publisher before he left West Point, and *Poems by Edgar A. Poe, Second Edition,* was issued by Elam Bliss sometime in April 1831. It had a long critical essay as a preface and was dedicated "to the U. S. Corps of Cadets."

In the preface Poe, strongly influenced by Coleridge's definition of poetry, used some of his words and then went on with a further definition of his own: "A poem, in my opinion, is opposed to a work of science by having for its *immediate* object pleasure, not truth." Then he explained that a poem is opposed "to romance by having for its object an *indefinite* instead of a *definite* pleasure; romance presenting perceptible images with definite, poetry with indefinite sensations, to which end music is an essential, since the comprehension of sweet sound is our most indefinite conception."

The little volume was reviewed in a few words in the *New York Mirror* and in even fewer in the Philadelphia *Saturday Evening Post*. It was Poe's third book, but its sales were negligible. Yet it contained poems that are far more mature than anything he had yet written. "Israfel," "The Valley of Unrest," and "The City in the Sea" first appeared in this collection. So did this, one of Poe's finest poems:

TO HELEN

Helen, thy beauty is to me
  Like those Nicéan barks of yore,
That gently, o'er a perfumed sea,
  The weary, way-worn wanderer bore
  To his own native shore.

On desperate seas long wont to roam,
  Thy hyacinth hair, thy classic face,
Thy Naiad airs have brought me home
  To the glory that was Greece,
  And the grandeur that was Rome.

Lo! in yon brilliant window-niche
  How statue-like I see thee stand,
The agate lamp within thy hand!
  Ah, Psyche, from the regions which
  Are Holy-Land!

The second stanza is printed here as it appeared in the revised version of 1841. In the 1831 *Poems*, the famous lines about Greece and Rome were rather flat:

To the beauty of fair Greece
And the grandeur of old Rome.

4

No Money...No Friends...
No Prospects

■✦✦✦✦✦✦✦✦✦✦✦✦✦✦✦✦✦✦✦✦✦✦✦✦✦✦✦✦✦✦✦✦✦✦✦✦✦✦✦■

I am ready to curse the day when I was born.
—LETTER TO JOHN ALLAN, October 16, 1831

While waiting for his third book of poems to appear, Poe was desperately trying to make up his mind about what he should do to earn a living. On March 10, he wrote a strange letter to Colonel Sylvanus Thayer, superintendent of West Point:

> Having no longer any ties which can bind me to my native country—no prospects—nor any friends—I intend . . . to proceed to Paris with the view of obtaining, thro' the interest of the Marquis de La Fayette, an appointment (if possible) in the Polish Army. In the event of the interference of France in behalf of Poland this may be easily effected—at all events it will be my only feasible plan of procedure.

A series of revolutions, beginning in France in 1830, had spread across Europe and had now reached Poland, where the Russians were trying to put the uprising down. Since France favored Poland, Poe hoped that Lafayette, whom he had met briefly in Richmond in 1824, would sponsor him for a commission as an officer in the Polish army. But nothing came of Poe's appeal, which was fortunate, because the Russians crushed the revolt before the year was out.

When *Poems, Second Edition,* came out, it got no better a reception than the two previous books, although it was far superior to them. Its disappointed author left New York and went to Baltimore where his aunt's already overcrowded house was open to him. There Mrs. Clemm; her young son, Henry; and even younger daughter, Virginia; Poe's grandmother; and his brother, William Henry Poe, lived in a state of near poverty. Virginia was then only eight years old.

Poe immediately tried to earn some money, for the family was largely dependent upon his grandmother's military pension of $20 a month. The city of Baltimore was then one of the most important cities in the country, and many publications were issued there. Poe's letters to them, however, brought no results, nor did his attempt to find a job as a schoolteacher.

Then, on June 4, *The Philadelphia Saturday Courier* printed a notice that offered $100 for the best short story received before December 1. The announcement caused Poe to shift his attention from poetry to prose. He promptly began to write a series of five stories, which were to be included in a book entitled *Tales of the Folio Club.*

The little group staying in Mrs. Clemm's house was reduced by one on August 1, when Poe's brother, William Henry, died at the age of twenty-four. Death seemed to be concentrating its attack on Baltimore, for a few weeks later, cholera struck the city. There was no protection from it. What Poe experienced during that dreadful epidemic later found expression in his stories "King Pest" and "The Masque of the Red Death," and in the prose poem "Shadow."

Perhaps the nearness of death in the stricken city caused Poe to regret his past life and the severance of his relationship with John Allan. On October 16 he wrote him a letter which was wholly unlike all his previous ones. It read, in part:

> . . . all communication seems to be at an end; and when I think of the twenty long years that I have called you father, and you have called me son, I could cry like a child to think that it should all end in this . . . . It is only at such a time as the present when I can write to you with the consciousness of making no application for assistance, that I dare to open my heart, or speak one word of old affection. When I look back upon the past and think of everything—of how much you tried to do for me—of your forbearance and generosity, in spite of the most flagrant ingratitude on my part, I can not help thinking myself the greatest fool in existence. I am ready to curse the day when I was born.

Although no letter of reply from Allan exists, he is believed to have sent one. But within a few weeks, Poe, who had proudly ended his letter to Allan with the statement that although wretchedly poor, he was out of debt, was again in trouble. He had been arrested (but not jailed) for a debt which, he said, had been incurred as much on his dead brother's account as on his own. He wrote to Allan, addressing him as "My Dear Pa," and begging for $80 to help him stay out of prison.

Allan did not answer; being dunned again was too much. Mrs. Clemm wrote to him, saying that she had been able to raise $20, but that was not enough to keep Poe out of the debtors' jail. Allan's reaction to the pleas for money was complicated. He was moved enough to write to a friend in Baltimore to advance Poe the needed sum and $20 extra, but he put his letter away unmailed. After two more pathetic notes from Poe, he took the letter to the post office and mailed it himself.

Despite his troubles, Poe went on writing his five stories for the *Saturday Courier*. He met the December 1 deadline, but he did not win the $100 prize. It was awarded to Delia S. Bacon, who had submitted a sentimental tale entitled "Love's Martyr." She was later to become known as a supporter of the theory that the plays ascribed to Shakespeare were actually written by Bacon, Raleigh, and Spenser. She died insane, and her work is forgotten.

But the *Courier* was enough impressed by Poe's stories to publish all five of them during the year 1832. He may not even have seen them in print, for they did not bear his name, and he almost certainly was not paid for them. "Metzengerstein," the best one, appeared in January.

This is not one of Poe's better stories, but it contains many elements that were to characterize his fiction. The setting is European; the central figure is dominated by his own passions; the supernatural is called upon; and after much suspense, the plot builds to a dramatic climax.

The other four stories—"The Duc de l'Omelette," "A Tale of Jerusalem," "A Decided Loss" (later entitled "Loss of Breath"), and "The Bargain Lost" (later "Bon-Bon")—

are all inferior to "Metzengerstein," and are seldom read to-day. They, too, have foreign settings.

With these, Poe began his career as a writer of fiction. There were very few authors of serious short stories in America then. Only Washington Irving, in his *Sketch Book* (1819–1820), had published any worth remembering—"Rip Van Winkle" and "The Legend of Sleepy Hollow." Hawthorne had had one story printed, but was as yet unknown, while Melville was still a young boy. Nathaniel Parker Willis was beginning to publish stories, but his light, inconsequential work did not survive him. As a magazine editor, however, he befriended Poe.

And Poe needed friendly magazine editors. Lack of copyright protection meant that American book publishers could bring out popular fiction by famous foreign authors without having to pay royalties or even to ask for permission. This naturally made it hard for an American writer to find a medium for his work. Journals, magazines, and annuals paid badly for short nonfiction pieces, but they usually paid something. Poe, like nearly every other author in this country, was forced to depend upon them.

As a result, the American fiction that did appear in the first half of the nineteenth century was rather poor. The relatively few novels and short stories that did get published seldom earned a living for their authors, and the writing of fiction was considered a hobby rather than a serious profession. Under such discouraging conditions it was only natural that would-be writers turned to other fields.

Little is known about Poe during the year 1832, although romantic rumors later had it that he was in Europe. It is not impossible that he again spent some time in the Army during this shadowy period, although positive proof is lacking. One thing is certain: he continued to write stories and completed six more of them. He was probably still living in Baltimore, for on August 4, 1832, the *Baltimore Saturday Visiter* printed a notice saying that its editor had read some of the new tales. He praised them highly and promised to print some of them, but he never did.

By April 12, 1832, Poe's situation had become so bad that he again appealed to John Allan for help: "I am perishing—absolutely perishing for want of aid. And yet I am not idle—nor addicted to any vice—nor have I committed any offence against society which would render me deserving of so hard a fate. For God's sake pity me, and save me from destruction."

With this despairing cry, Poe's correspondence with John Allan ends. Again there was no answer.

Painful as it had been for Poe to beg his foster father for funds, it had at least sometimes been possible to obtain a little much-needed money from him. Now, with no job, no prospects, and no cash on hand, Poe was haunted by his poverty. When he offered a manuscript to a New England publisher in the spring of 1833, he added the postscript: "I am poor."

During this spring, Mrs. Clemm moved her little household to No. 3 Amity Street (now No. 203). The two-story brick building was incredibly small and undoubtedly cheap to rent.

A month after Poe's last letter to Allan, he had eleven stories ready for the collection he intended to call *Tales of the*

Folio Club. He even wrote an introduction for the book.
Over a period of time, he changed the title several times. He
next called it *Eleven Tales of the Arabesque* and then *Tales
of the Grotesque and Arabesque.* When it was finally published at the end of 1839 with an 1840 date, it included
twenty-five stories and was issued in two volumes.

Poe never gave up hope of seeing his prose fiction printed
in book form. Meanwhile, he continued to write story after
story, some of indifferent quality, and a few that are still read
throughout the world.

His immediate problem was to get his work published in
magazines. His chance came in June 1833 when the *Baltimore
Saturday Visiter,* which had already praised his work, announced a prize contest of $50. Poe submitted his six latest
tales, and in October received a letter telling him that he had
won the prize with "MS. Found in a Bottle."

With this story, Poe earned his first money from fiction.
He was only twenty-four years old, but he was already becoming a serious writer. The tale deals with a man who was ship-
wrecked in a typhoon and who found himself accidentally
cast aboard a phantom vessel that was rapidly sailing toward
an Antarctic maelstrom. In this, it resembles his later "A
Descent into the Maelström." Poe was always fascinated by
deep places whether on land or sea. Graves, pits, and whirl-
pools play prominent parts in his writings.

One of the three judges of the contest many years later
described Poe as he was at this time:

> He carried himself erect and well, as one who was trained
> to it. [His years in the Army and West Point had taught him

that.] He was dressed in black, and his frockcoat was but-
toned to the throat, where it met the black stock, then almost
universally worn. Not a particle of white was visible. Coat,
hat, boots, and gloves had very evidently seen their best days,
but so far as mending and brushing go, everything had been
done, apparently, to make them presentable. On most men
his clothes would have looked shabby and seedy, but there
was something about this man that prevented one from criti-
cizing his garments.

Another of the judges, John Pendleton Kennedy, a well-
to-do lawyer who wrote fiction under the name Mark Little-
ton, befriended Poe. He helped him get in touch with publishers and was one of the few influential men who ever did
anything for the fiercely proud young writer who alienated
most people.

Sometime early in 1834, Poe went to Richmond and
called at the Allan house to see his foster father, who was now
so ill with dropsy that he had to sleep sitting up in a chair.
According to the only account there is of this visit, when the
second Mrs. Allan answered the doorbell, Poe pushed past her
and went upstairs to the invalid's room. Allan shook his cane
at him and ordered him out of the house.

It was their last meeting, for Allan died on March 27. In
his will, he provided for his illegitimate children but left nothing at all to his foster son.

There are few known facts about Poe's life for the rest of
the year, but he must have been busy writing, for several new
stories were published during the spring of 1835. As usual, he
was miserably poor. During that spring, he asked Kennedy to

help him get work as a public school teacher, but he did not obtain a position. And when Kennedy invited him to dinner, his reply shows how absolutely destitute he was: "I cannot come—and for reasons of the most humiliating nature in my personal appearance. . . . If you will be my friend so far as to loan me $20, I will call on you to-morrow—otherwise it will be impossible, and I must submit to my fate."

Kennedy was obviously moved by this letter. Years later he wrote in his journal that he had found Poe "in a state of starvation. I gave him clothing, free access to my table and the use of a horse for exercise whenever he chose; in fact brought him up from the very verge of despair."

Kennedy was able to get four of Poe's stories published in the *Southern Literary Messenger*, which had recently been started in Richmond. Two of them—"Berenice" and "Morella"—deal with Poe's favorite theme, the death of a beautiful young woman. In "Berenice" the plot rises to a powerful but somewhat ridiculous climax. "Morella" is more sensible, but both tales are just steps on the way to one of Poe's greatest stories, "Ligeia," which was not published until 1838.

If it seems strange that American readers were willing to tolerate these tales of horror in an age that was noted for its conventionality, it must be remembered that Poe's audience had been prepared for them by the many Gothic tales of terror which had been popular in Europe and America for more than half a century. Poe was not the first to enter this field; he had been preceded by the English writers Horace Walpole, Ann Radcliffe, and Matthew Gregory ("Monk") Lewis, the German author E. T. A. Hoffmann, and the American novelist Charles Brockden Brown. Poe just proved to be better at this kind of writing than anyone else and made it particularly his own.

One of Poe's nonhorror stories published in the *Messenger* that spring was "The Unparalleled Adventures of One Hans Pfaall." In this, Poe, who was to originate so many things, became one of the first to write science fiction, for it is about an imaginary trip to the moon. This was his first hoax; there were to be others.

Although Poe was now busy perfecting his ability to write short stories, he did not neglect his first love—poetry. He continued to write verse, although he found it increasingly difficult to get his poems published. On several occasions he inserted them into his stories just to see them appear in print. "To One in Paradise," "Hymn," "Latin Hymn," "Song of Triumph," were first presented to readers in this way. But the poem entitled "The Coliseum" reversed the process. It was printed in the *Baltimore Saturday Visiter* and was later woven into Poe's only play, the verse-tragedy "Politian," which he was writing during the year 1835.

FROM "THE COLISEUM"

Here, where a hero fell, a column falls!
Here, where the mimic eagle glared in gold,
A midnight vigil holds the swarthy bat!
Here, where the dames of Rome their gilded hair
Waved to the wind, now wave the reed and thistle!
Here, where on golden throne the monarch lolled,
Glides, spectre-like, unto his marble home,
Lit by the wan light of the hornéd moon,
The swift and silent lizard of the stones!

5

Richmond Again – and Marriage

■ ✦✦✦ ■

Hear the mellow wedding bells—
Golden bells!
—"THE BELLS," 1849

In addition to stories and poems, the *Southern Literary Messenger* also published book reviews by Poe. As a reviewer, he was often ruthless. He had received his training in this work by a careful reading of periodicals like *Blackwood's Edinburgh Magazine*, which was noted for the savage attacks its editors made on the books they wrote about.

Such harsh notices were not in keeping with the gentlemanly policy of the *Messenger*, but its owner, Thomas Willis White, tolerated them because he was a poorly-educated printer who needed someone like Poe to write for his rather colorless journal. And, as he soon found out, the vitriolic notices brought the paper nationwide attention and increased circulation.

This was also true of other forms of writing that Poe did

for the *Messenger*. When White complained about "Berenice" being "far too horrible" and therefore in bad taste, Poe wrote to him at length to explain his attitude about such work. "To be appreciated," he said, "you must be *read*, and these things are invariably sought after with great avidity." He then proposed to furnish the magazine with a similar tale every month and added shrewdly: "The effect—if any—will be estimated better by the circulation of the Magazine than by any comments upon its contents."

The once-naïve young poet was rapidly becoming a professional journalist, cynical about his readers, and more than willing to supply them with the horror stories he was sure they wanted.

White needed Poe, and Poe needed White. Payments of $5 and $4.94 for contributions to the May issue were very welcome in the poverty-stricken little house on Baltimore's Amity Street, where someone (including Poe) always seemed to be ailing and the 79-year-old grandmother was dying. Her monthly pension of $20 was essential for the family's existence, and everyone dreaded the idea of her passing away, but she had been bedridden for eight years and was paralyzed.

Sometime in June, White asked Poe if he would come to Richmond to do some proofreading and other journalistic tasks. Poe said that he would be glad to. In his letter he made some suggestions for improving the typography of the *Messenger* which were adopted later that year.

Poe's grandmother died on July 7, and the all-important pension came to an end. At some time during the next few weeks, Poe went to Richmond, to stay for a month while he earned a little money by working for the *Messenger*.

While there, he was utterly miserable. He missed Mrs. Clemm and Virginia and felt very much alone. Again he took to drink to forget a feeling of depression that was almost overwhelming. He was sober enough on August 20 to reply to William Poe, a second cousin living in Augusta, Georgia, who had written a letter of condolence shortly after the grandmother had died. In his letter, Poe summarized the family history as he knew it. Describing his own career, he distorted the truth but revealed several interesting things about himself. "Brought up to no profession, and educated in the expectation of an immense fortune (Mr. A. having been worth $750,000) the blow has been a heavy one." And then he said that he had "lately obtained the Editorship of the Southern Messenger," which, of course, was not true, because he was only a minor employee. Despite the impressive title he gave to himself, he urged William Poe to come to the assistance of Mrs. Clemm and her two children who were now in even worse straits than usual.

Meanwhile, Neilson Poe, another cousin, had offered to take 13-year-old Virginia off Mrs. Clemm's hands and bring her up in his own family. When Poe heard of this, he was absolutely heartbroken, as his letter of August 29 to Mrs. Clemm shows:

My Dearest Aunty,
    I am blinded with tears while writing this letter—I have no wish to live another hour . . . . You well know how little I am able to bear up under the pressure of grief—My bitterest enemy would pity me could he now read my heart—My last my last my only hold on life is cruelly torn away—I have no desire to live and *will not*. But let my duty be done. I love,

you know I love Virginia passionately devotedly. I cannot express in words the fervent devotion I feel towards my dear little cousin—my own darling . . . . It is useless to disguise the truth that when Virginia goes with N. P. that I shall never behold her again—that is absolutely sure. Pity me, my dear Aunty, pity me. I have no one now to fly to—I am among strangers, and my wretchedness is more than I can bear. It is useless to expect advice from me—what can I say? Can I, in honour and in truth say—Virginia! do not go! do not go where you can be comfortable and perhaps happy—and on the other hand can I calmly resign my—life itself[?] If she had truly loved me would she not have rejected the offer with scorn? Oh God have mercy on me! If she goes with N. P. what are you to do, my own Aunty,?

I had procured a sweet little house in a retired situation on Church Hill—newly done up and with a large garden and every convenience—at only $5 per month. I have been dreaming every day and night since of the rapture I should feel in having my only friends—all I love on Earth with me there, [and] the pride I would take in making you both comfortable and in calling her my wife—But the dream is over. Oh God have mercy on me. What have I to live for? Among strangers with not one soul to love me . . . .

White was engaged to make my salary $60 a month, and we could live in comparative comfort and happiness—even the $4 a week I am now paying for board would support us all—but I shall have $15 a week, and what need would we have of more? . . .

The tone of your letter wounds me to the soul. Oh Aunty, Aunty you loved me once—how can you be so cruel now? You speak of Virginia acquiring accomplishments, and entering into society—you speak in so worldly a tone. Are you sure she would be more happy? Do you think any one could love her more dearly than I? She will have far—very far better opportunities of entering society here than with N. P. Every one here receives me with open arms.

Adieu my dear Aunty. I *cannot advise* you. Ask Virginia. Leave it to her. Let me have, under her own hand, a letter, bidding me *good bye*—forever—and I may die—my heart will break—but I will say no more. Kiss her for me—a million times.

For Virginia,

My love, my own sweetest Sissy, my darling little wifey, think well before you break the heart of your cousin, Eddy.

In this emotion-laden letter, one of the most moving in a correspondence that is noted for its never-ceasing anguish, Poe set down for the first time the love he had for Virginia.

Poe's pressing need for money made him eloquent, for he was able to persuade White to employ him at a salary of $10 a week. White, however, had reservations which he expressed in a letter to one of his advisors on September 8, when he said that Poe was not editor and that he "could place very little reliance upon him" because he was "unfortunately rather dissipated." He added, though, that "his disposition is quite amiable."

One might think that having a regular income would have eased Poe's mind, but it did not. He was more distraught than ever, as he admitted in a letter to his friend and sponsor, John P. Kennedy: "I am suffering under a depression of spirits such as I have never felt before. . . . I am wretched, and I know not why. . . . Convince me that it is worth one's while

—that it is at all necessary to live, and you will prove yourself indeed my friend."

But Poe, despite his misery, never forgot that he was a writer and that he also wanted to be an editor. At the end of his letter he asked Kennedy if he had a contribution that he could send to the *Messenger* and then went on at some length about his own stories. He said that White had offered to publish his *Tales of the Folio Club* but asked Kennedy to find out from Carey and Lea, the well-known Philadelphia firm, whether they would be willing to take books printed by White and bring them out under their own imprint.

There was more trouble with White. On September 21, he told a friend that Poe had left Richmond and added: "His habits are not good. He is in addition the victim of melancholia. I should not be at all astonished to hear that he had been guilty of suicide."

It was not, however, suicide but marriage that Poe sought. He had gone to Baltimore, won Mrs. Clemm's consent, and on September 22 taken out a license to wed Virginia. It may be that he actually did marry her secretly at this time, but there is no record of it. She was then hardly more than 13 years old.

Those who knew Virginia described her as a delicate-looking young creature with a soft round face, dark eyes, dark hair, and very white skin. There was a trace of a lisp in her voice, and she was retiring and shy. They all say that she moved with grace and beauty, and that she had "an air of refinement and good breeding." Her one accomplishment was music, and she was learning to play the piano and sing. She was easily moved to tears, and on one occasion she burst out crying when she saw a stranger's funeral. She had never gone to school; she got the little education she had from Poe.

Late in September, White wrote a long, fatherly letter to Poe:

> How much I regretted parting with you is unknown to any one on this earth, except myself. I was attached to you—and am still—and willingly would I say return, if I did not dread the hour of separation very shortly again.
>
> You have fine talents, Edgar, and you ought to have them respected. . . . Separate yourself from the bottle, and bottle companions, for ever! . . .
>
> If you should come to Richmond again, and again should be my assistant in my office, it must be especially understood by us that all engagements on my part would be dissolved the moment you get drunk. . . . No man is safe who drinks before breakfast! No man can do so and attend to business properly.

Poe thought that the presence of Virginia and Mrs. Clemm would help matters, so he brought them to Richmond early in October and set them up in a boardinghouse on Capitol Square. He persuaded White to take him back and was soon hard at work again.

As a result of his absences, there was no issue of the *Messenger* for October, and the November number did not come out until December. Yet Poe's work, much of it unsigned, now covered columns in the paper.

In it he was able to publish part of his long poem, "Politian," as well as some short poems and stories, most of which, however, were revised versions of earlier writing that had already appeared in other papers.

He wrote a great many book reviews, some of them savage and satiric. One, directed at a novel written by an editor of the *New-York Mirror*, attracted wide attention but also brought Poe into disfavor with the powerful group of New York authors and publishers.

During this time, Poe was beginning to be interested in writing serious criticism; he also wove analyses of the nature of poetry into the text of some of his book reviews. In the April 1836 issue of the *Messenger*, when he dealt with two books by Joseph Rodman Drake and Fitz-Greene Halleck, he wrote one of the first well-thought-out definitions of poetry to appear in American literature:

> Poetry has never been defined to the satisfaction of all parties. Perhaps, in the present condition of language it never will be. Words cannot hem it in. Its intangible and purely spiritual nature refuses to be bound down within the widest horizon of mere sounds. But it is not, therefore, misunderstood—at least, not by all men is it misunderstood. Very far from it. If, indeed, there be any one circle of thought distinctly and palpably marked out from amid the jarring and tumultuous chaos of human intelligence, it is that evergreen and radiant Paradise which the true poet knows, and knows alone, as the limited realm of his authority—as the circumscribed Eden of his dreams. But a definition is a thing of words—a conception of ideas. And thus while we readily believe that Poesy, the term, it will be troublesome, if not impossible to define—still, with its image vividly existing in the world, we apprehend no difficulty in so describing Poesy, the Sentiment, as to imbue even the most obtuse intellect with a comprehension of it sufficiently distinct for all the purposes of practical analysis. . . .

Poesy is the sentiment of Intellectual Happiness here, and the Hope of a higher Intellectual Happiness hereafter.

Imagination is its soul. With the *passions* of mankind—although it may modify them greatly—although it may exalt, or inflame, or purify, or control them—it would require little ingenuity to prove that it has no inevitable, and indeed no necessary co-existence.

This April issue of the *Messenger* also contained Poe's first venture into a field for which he was to become world-famous, for "Maelzel's Chess-Player" is really the first step on the way to his invention of the detective story.

The Chess Player was a life-sized figure of a Turk seated at a table on which there was a chess board. Its supposedly mechanical left hand could move the pieces and win time after time—but not all the time—against opponents who volunteered to compete against it. This automaton had been invented in Germany in 1769 and later brought to America by J. N. Maelzel, who exhibited it in various cities.

In his article, Poe told the story of the figure's past, and then, by the deductive reasoning which was to make his detective stories possible, showed how it could not be an automaton but was actually a hollow shape in which a highly skilled chess player could hide himself, view the board, and make the moves with the dummy's left hand.

Since Carey and Lea had declined to publish Poe's collected short stories, he submitted them to Harper and Brothers, who also rejected them. Their reasons for doing so are interesting. First, they said, because some of the tales had already appeared in print; second, because they were short, and long experience had taught them that readers in this country wanted only book-length fiction; and third, because the stories were "too learned and mystical."

Thus one of the longest-lived books in American literature was sent back to its author.

On May 16, 1836, Poe applied for a marriage bond, which was put into effect that evening, when a Presbyterian service was performed in the boardinghouse, and Poe and Virginia Eliza Clemm, who was not yet 14 years old, were officially wed. The newly-married couple went to nearby Petersburg for a short honeymoon. There they were welcomed by the editor of the local newspaper. They seem to have been happy even though this was Virginia's first separation from her mother.

When they returned to Richmond, they found that a house which White had bought for Mrs. Clemm to use for boarders was too small even for two families. Poe was in trouble again, for he had borrowed $200 to buy furniture. Again he turned to Kennedy for help, but did not get any. He also tried to persuade an attorney to enter a suit against the Federal Government for compensation for money spent by his grandfather to aid the Revolution. This, too, proved to be fruitless.

Now that Poe had a young wife and her mother to provide for, he worked harder than ever and got a promise from White to increase his salary from $15 to $20 a week in November. But things never ran smoothly in the Poe family, for a few days after the promised increase, White gave Poe notice and then reinstated him.

Yet the August number was a very good one, filled with material which Poe had written. One of his reviews dealt with suggestions for an expedition to chart the Pacific Ocean. These had been made by Jeremiah N. Reynolds, a now-forgotten explorer whose books inspired Melville to write *Moby-Dick*. He had a lifelong effect on Poe, whose story "MS. Found in a Bottle" owed some of its ideas to Reynolds. Another American writer, John Cleve Symmes, who had some strange notions about the earth being open at the poles and hollow with people living inside, also influenced Poe.

It was about this time that Poe began to write his only book-length work of fiction, *The Narrative of Arthur Gordon Pym*. What Harper's had said about the American public preferring long stories to short ones was now being taken as sound advice.

Although *Pym* is a sea story with all sorts of adventures, including shipwreck, storms, mutiny, starvation and cannibalism, as well as encounters with savage tribes, it is actually more than that. In it, Poe expresses in narrative form the dark forebodings and the inner struggles that dominated his life. It is filled with symbolism and strange images that disguise much that he could not—and would not—say openly about himself. Since much of it comes from an unconscious level, he did not realize what he was putting down on paper for future generations to interpret.

Like Melville's *Moby-Dick*, which was published half a generation later, *Pym* can first be read for its adventurous plot and can then be studied later for the rich treasures of the imagination that are concealed within it.

As a published novel, however, *The Narrative of Arthur*

Gordon Pym was not a success. Oddly enough, it did better in England than in the United States. In both countries, some reviewers thought that the book was supposed to be a true account of sea voyages and criticized its author for exaggerating some of its obviously invented incidents.

Poe continued to write much of the *Messenger's* text, but his relations with White were getting worse. Again the November issue came out in December. Late that month White told a friend that he was going to give his editor a week's notice. There is no doubt that Poe had been drinking again; he admitted as much a few years later. But White resented Poe's greater ability, while Poe called White "an illiterate and vulgar, although well-meaning man, who had neither the capacity to appreciate my labors, nor the will to reward them."

The January 1837 issue of the *Messenger* carried a polite notice that Poe's editorial duties were ceasing with that number, although he continued to work for it for most of the month.

White had now had enough of Poe. In a letter to a friend he said, "I am as sick of his writings as I am of him . . . . and am rather more than half inclined to send him up another dozen dollars in the morning, and along with it all his unpublished manuscripts." Nevertheless, the January and February issues carried the first two installments of *The Narrative of Arthur Gordon Pym*, which then abruptly stopped.

During Poe's brief stay with the *Southern Literary Messenger*, the circulation increased from 500 to 3500 copies. Since the population of Richmond was then only about 20,000, it is obvious that the magazine was going far beyond the borders of the city or even of the state of Virginia. But its owner was unwilling to give complete authority or recognition to the brilliant editor who was making his paper nationally known. And Poe, fully aware that he was much superior to the man who employed him, could no longer stand being subordinated to a person for whom he had lost all respect.

Despite the fact that he had no savings or assets, he was nevertheless ready to make his next move. He now felt quite sure that Richmond was too small for him. He wanted a larger territory to operate in, even though most people thought that his career with the *Messenger* had been a failure.

The judgment of time is against them, however, for White, his friends, his other writers, and the *Messenger* are remembered only because of their association with the poorly paid, little-appreciated editor who was making a name for himself that would outlast time.

6

New Fields to Conquer

■✦✦■

Terror is not of Germany but of the soul.

—PREFACE TO *Tales of the Grotesque and Arabesque*, 1839–1840

New York was then the largest city in the United States, and, more important to Poe, it was the nation's publishing center. Perhaps the fact that he wanted Harper's to issue *The Narrative of Arthur Gordon Pym* caused him to move there. Now that he was free from editorial work, he could concentrate on his long sea story.

Sometime in February 1837, he, Virginia, and Mrs. Clemm arrived in downtown New York, almost surely by ship, for that was then the usual way to travel from one seacoast city to another. They settled in Greenwich Village, where Mrs. Clemm opened a boardinghouse. One of its patrons, who eventually became a bookseller, was so favorably impressed by Poe and his family that he later wrote an account of his memories of them. He said that Poe never got drunk, and "was one

of the most courteous, gentlemanly, and intelligent companions I have met with." And also that Virginia was surpassingly
lovely and devoted to her husband.

While in New York, Poe sold two short stories and was
given a chance to review the first travel book written by John
Lloyd Stephens, who became one of the most noted explorers
and archaeologists of nineteenth-century America. This book,
dealing with his travels in the Near East, was obviously worthy
of an extended article, and Poe did it full justice. He got in
touch with Professor Charles Anthon of Columbia College
for background information, and with his help was able to
write an informed review of the Stephens book. Meanwhile,
he spent most of his time working on the manuscript of *Pym*.

Poe could not have chosen a worse time to come to New
York. As a reviewer, he was sometimes unduly severe even in
an age that was noted for the harshness of its criticism. Since
he was clever with words, he could write a cutting phrase that
won chuckles from readers but offended the luckless author
whose work was being noticed. Even worse, he would often
go on at great length to demolish a trivial book that obviously
was not worth the time and effort he gave it. As a result, he
had already antagonized several of New York's more powerful
editors, most of whom did some writing of their own.

In addition to this, 1837 was the beginning of a financial
panic. There had been rumblings of economic difficulties early
in the year, then in May all the New York banks were forced
to suspend specie payment. More than 600 banks throughout
the country failed during the next few months, and a seven-
year depression began.

Harper's, however, was a very strong house. They read

the chapters of *Pym*, which Poe had finished, and copyrighted them in June even though they were not to issue the book for another year. The Panic of 1837 may have had something to do with the delay. Poe based his real events in *Pym* on books he had read about the South Seas, but the fictional parts are the best, particularly those that have to do with mystery and horror.

The winter of 1837–1838 was a miserable one, and it was only the tiny income from Mrs. Clemm's boardinghouse that kept the little family alive. Late that spring they decided to move to Philadelphia. It was an important city, only slightly smaller than New York, and it, too, was a major publishing center. And, just as Harper's had acted like a magnet to draw Poe to New York, the firm of Carey and Lea was attracting him to Philadelphia. So were periodicals like *Burton's Gentleman's Magazine*, *Godey's Lady's Book*, and the *Saturday Evening Post*.

Harper's published *Pym* in July 1838, and the move to Philadelphia was made about that time. Poe was—or had been—working on one of his finest stories, "Ligeia," for he acknowledged $10 in payment for it in a letter written on September 4 to an editor of Baltimore's new *American Museum of Literature and the Arts*. It appeared in the first number, September 1838. "Ligeia" was the ultimate development of the death-of-a-beautiful-woman theme which had begun with "Berenice" and "Morella" a few years before.

The Poes lived in several places in Philadelphia, usually in small private houses, which were all they could afford, for the money problem was as pressing as ever. When a free-lance editorial assignment paying $50 was offered, Poe gladly took it, even though the work was very different from anything he had ever done. His task was to put together a textbook on shells. He explained his connection with the book a number of years later:

> I wrote it in conjunction with Professor Thomas Wyatt and Professor McMurtrie . . . my name being put to the work as best known and most likely to aid its circulation. I wrote the Preface and the Introduction, and translated from Cuvier the accounts of the animals, etc. All school-books are necessarily made in a similar way.

By agreement, Poe paraphrased most of the text from Wyatt's already published *Conchology*, but he also took much of the material—not by agreement—from a book by Thomas Brown which had been issued in Scotland in 1833. As a result, charges of plagiarism were made against Poe and hung over his head for years. Fortunately, *The Conchologist's First Book, or a System of Testaceous Malachology*, although it carries Poe's name, and only his, on the title page, has very little to do with Poe as a writer. Oddly enough, it is the only book bearing his name that was reprinted in America while he was still alive, although *Pym* went through several editions in England. When the third edition of the book on shells came out in 1845, Poe's name was no longer on it.

Even though Poe knew that he was wasting his time doing work like this, he had to earn a living. Meanwhile, he was writing some of his best poetry. "The Haunted Palace" with its fearful ending

> A hideous throng rush out forever
> And laugh—but smile no more

was published in the *American Museum* in April 1839. Poe had the good sense to include the poem in one of his very finest and best-known stories, "The Fall of the House of Usher," which appeared in *Burton's Gentleman's Magazine* in September.

It was natural that it should be printed there, for Poe had written to the magazine's publisher, William E. Burton, applying for editorial work, and in May had been employed at a salary of $10 a week for only two hours of work a day. "Usher" was followed in October by "William Wilson."

Poe's name appeared as an editor of the magazine starting with the June issue. He evidently was getting on well with Burton, although he received a letter from him at the end of May chiding him for being too harsh in his book reviews. This letter, with forged sentences inserted and published posthumously, was to play a part in the maligning of Poe's reputation by his literary executor, Rufus W. Griswold.

Late in September, Poe at last achieved what he had long wanted. He got a letter from Lea and Blanchard (formerly Carey and Lea) saying that they were willing to publish at their own risk a small edition of his tales in two volumes. The profit, if any, was to be theirs, but he would retain the copyright, and be given a few copies for distribution to his friends. He was to receive no money at all.

Nevertheless, he was delighted that twenty-five of his stories were to be issued in book form. He knew all too well how ephemeral the magazines of his day were. But books live on, pass from reader to reader, and long outlast their authors.

Tales of the Grotesque and Arabesque was published in December 1839, although the title page bears the date 1840.

Even before the book appeared, Poe's work was receiving praise from prominent writers. A letter had come from England written by Isaac Disraeli, author of the widely read *Curiosities of Literature* and father of the even more famous Benjamin. Washington Irving also wrote to say how much he admired "The Fall of the House of Usher."

According to Poe, his two-volume collection of tales was given "the very highest possible praise" by the Philadelphia journals. He expected little from Baltimore, because his cousin, Neilson Poe, was editor of a daily newspaper there, and Poe mistakenly believed that Neilson was his enemy.

Only 750 copies of the *Tales* were printed, and they were slow to move. A few weeks after publication, Poe said that the edition was nearly exhausted, but he was mistaken. Publication of the book did him some good, but it was impossible for him, of course, to make any money out of it.

In the preface to the *Tales*, Poe, who had often been irritated by the frequently-made statement that his work was filled with "Germanism and gloom," countered the accusation by saying that the terror in his stories was "not of Germany but of the soul." He explained, although not very clearly, that "Arabesques" are conjured up by a vivid imagination and that "Grotesques" are likely to have ludicrous, satirical, or mock-heroic aspects. This is interesting, for both words used in these senses are ignored by all dictionaries. To the modern reader, Poe's *Grotesques* are likely to seem silly and outdated. Examples of them are such seldom-read tales as "Four Beasts in One," "The Man That Was Used Up," "Never Bet the Devil Your Head," "The Spectacles," and "Why the Little Frenchman Wears His Hand in a Sling." Savage buffoonery may have appealed to an audience then, but today these stories seem repulsive. One of them, "Hop-Frog," is a vengeful tale about a crippled court jester. Fortunately, it does not try to be funny and therefore succeeds brilliantly in its murderous fury. Undoubtedly, there is much of Poe in the dwarf who finally struck back at his high-placed enemies.

By this time in his career, Poe had become restless and wanted to start a magazine of his own in which he would be able to do whatever he wished and not be under the thumb of an employer whose taste and ability he despised. Burton, in some ways, was better than White, but both men lacked creative ability, critical judgment, and vision. Poe makes several references to such an ideal magazine as early as the autumn of 1839. They were to become more frequent as he gained more confidence in himself and saw how vastly inferior to him his employers were.

In the same month that *Tales* was published (December 1839), Poe inserted a notice in *Alexander's Weekly Messenger* offering to solve any cryptograms readers might send in. He got a surprising number of answers from places as far away as Alabama, Massachusetts, and Iowa. For fifteen issues the *Weekly Messenger* continued to print Poe's articles on secret writing and his solutions to the enciphered messages received.

This was at a time when cryptography was almost unknown in America, so Poe was a pioneer in the field. His mind was exceedingly good in applying logical reasoning to any abstract problem. He had first showed signs of this in 1836 with the publication of "Maelzel's Chess-Player." His interest in ciphers and codes was a further development of the same process of logical reasoning, which was soon to lead to his invention of the detective story. There were at least two Poes: one, the sensitive poet and writer of highly imaginative fiction; the other, a cool, objective appraiser of situations that had to be dealt with by analysis and deduction. The two were tied together by the inventiveness common to them both.

Eighteen months after Poe first challenged *Alexander's* readers to send in ciphers, he placed an article entitled "A Few Words on Secret Writing" in *Graham's Magazine* in which he discussed cryptography as it then stood and made some suggestions for improving it. He also stated that "human ingenuity cannot concoct a cipher which human ingenuity cannot resolve." This was true in his day and for many years afterward, but in recent times the art of enciphering a secret message has changed completely. Now, with electronic devices, some of them so hush-hush that descriptions of them have not reached the public, the secrecy of the message is said to be unbreakable.

It was no coincidence that Poe and his readers were interested in ciphers at this time, for it was then that Samuel F. B. Morse was inventing the electric telegraph, which had to use dots and dashes in place of letters. Messages that came over the wires could not be read by the average person because he could not understand either the first mysterious symbols marked on a moving strip of tape or the rapid chatter of the later receiving instruments. Only a trained operator could reduce these to letters and words.

During the first six months of 1840, Poe anonymously published installments of his projected *Journal of Julius Rod-*

man in *Burton's Gentleman's Magazine.* It is a fictitious account of the first passage across the Rocky Mountains and is Poe's only venture into the American West. He never finished it, because he had what was reported to be a drunken quarrel with Burton.

In a long letter to Burton, written on May 30, 1840, Poe analyzed their financial arrangement and showed how it had worked to his disadvantage. During the past year he had written an average of nearly 11 pages a month for the magazine. At the usual rate of $3 a page, his writings alone were surely worth $33. This, deducted from his monthly salary of $50, left $17 a month or $4.25 a week for "proofreading, general superintendence at the printing office, reading, alteration and preparation of m.s.s." as well as doing certain articles. Poe had been badly paid, and he knew it. He also resented the fact that Burton had been planning to sell the magazine but had told him nothing about it. Burton now wanted to return to the theater, which was his major interest, and was eager to get out of the publishing business.

Under the circumstances, Poe felt that the hostility between him and Burton was too great for him to make a bid for the publication even if he could somehow manage to raise the money. Instead, he drew up a prospectus for the *Penn Magazine* and began to circulate this among influential people. He also made an appeal for subscribers to the proposed periodical. Oddly enough, he did obtain some names.

In September, Poe tried to find a job for a man named C. Auguste Dubouchet. Nothing is known about him except that his unusual and very French combination of names inspired Poe to call his immortal sleuth C. Auguste Dupin. And

Poe's ever-active mind was busy at this time with an idea that was soon to result in the world's first detective story.

At the end of the year, Burton sold his *Gentleman's Magazine* to George R. Graham, who wanted to combine it with another magazine, the *Casket*. A few months later, he changed the title of the combination to *Graham's Magazine*. It was with this new publication that Poe reached the height of his career as a writer and editor.

7

All Things Must Have an End

I do believe that Eblis hath
A snare in every human path.

—"Tamerlane," 1827–1845

The first number of the combined magazines was also the last issue of *Burton's* (December 1840). It carried a story by Poe entitled "The Man of the Crowd." This brief tale, with its superb description of the streets of nighttime London and its abruptly twisted ending, is seldom fully appreciated by the modern reader, yet it ranks among Poe's best psychological studies.

If Poe had been at least adequately paid and given more authority and respect by the two magazine owners he had worked for, he might have been content to be a salaried editor for the rest of his life. He did not care about earning large sums of money, and the only power he sought was freedom for the publication of his writings. His keen intelligence told him that all the American magazines then in existence were poor things, unworthy of serious attention. He was certain that his own projected journal would be better than any yet published in this country. And it almost surely would have been.

Back in June 1840, he had enlarged his prospectus for the *Penn Magazine* and had copies of it printed. It promised that the new publication's book reviews would be less harsh than those that Poe had previously written although they would still be severe. On all subjects the monthly magazine would have "an honest and fearless opinion." Only "the best pens" were to write for it. Its chief aim was to please. It was to be illustrated "by the leading artists of the country," and its first number was scheduled to appear on January 1, 1841.

But Poe became ill, and the publication date was put off until March 1, 1841. He was convinced that the prospects for the *Penn* were "glorious," but it was impossible to get backing while the nation's banks were still in trouble. On April 1, Poe wrote sadly that his magazine was only "scotched, not killed." Meantime, he said, Graham had made him a liberal offer, and he was glad to get the employment. "The Penn project," he added, "will unquestionably be resumed hereafter."

Poe never gave up the idea of having his own magazine, although he was never able to start it. This was the world's loss, for he was a first-rate editor, one of the best in the United States. He was the victim of his time and place. Lack of an effective international copyright law made it difficult for an American writer to sell his work here, because famous foreign authors could be published in this country without the publisher having to pay royalties to them. As a result, popular books and short pieces published in the United States were largely of British origin. And an American author received nothing when his work was issued abroad.

George R. Graham, the publisher of *Graham's Magazine*, was four years younger than Poe. He was an energetic and ambitious young man who had begun his working career as a cabinetmaker; then he went on to study law. He became an assistant editor of Philadelphia's *Saturday Evening Post* and bought the *Casket* from it.

When he acquired *Burton's Gentleman's Magazine*, he had the good sense to realize that Poe had been one of its greatest assets. By April 1841, Graham was publishing Poe's book reviews and wanted him to work on the paper. Thus began one of the most pleasant associations in Poe's usually unhappy career.

The April issue of *Graham's* made history, for it contained "The Murders in the Rue Morgue," the world's first detective story. In it, Poe's C. Auguste Dupin set the pattern for dozens of later sleuths.

Dupin is, of course, one aspect of Poe himself. Here the sensitive poet and teller of imaginative tales is replaced by the brilliant thinker, a man who calls upon reason alone to solve crimes that baffle the police. The story opens with a long essay on the powers of analysis and goes on to state that the game of checkers (referred to as draughts) is intellectually superior to chess. After several pages of this, Dupin is introduced. The tale is told in the first person by a companion whose usefulness inspired Conan Doyle to create Dr. Watson, who serves as a similar mouthpiece for Sherlock Holmes. When Dupin solves the brutal murder in the Rue Morgue, he explains his chain of reasoning to his companion, just as Holmes does later to Watson.

The outstanding April 1841 issue of *Graham's* also contained a review by Poe of *Sketches of Conspicuous Characters of France*. In this he renewed the offer he had made in *Alexander's Weekly Messenger* in December 1839 to solve cryptograms. He now extended the offer to include messages written in French, Italian, Spanish, German, Latin, or Greek.

It was just about this time that Rufus W. Griswold, who was to be Poe's evil genius, entered his life. Griswold, the son of a poor Vermont farmer, was six years younger than Poe. He had had little education and got most of his training in various printshops. He had recently been licensed as a Baptist minister but apparently never had a pulpit. He used the degrees of D.D. and LL.D. after his name but did not explain how he had gained the right to use them.

He was working on a Philadelphia newspaper and also compiling *The Poets and Poetry of America* when he first met Poe. Poe, of course, was eager to see his work included in the projected anthology and was most cooperative. From then on, the two men's careers often ran parallel, although Griswold was only a compiler. He wanted to write both prose and poetry, but his work in those fields was mediocre. Lowell once said that he was "an ass, and what's more, a knave." Poe also had a poor opinion of him, but he realized that Griswold was a useful person for an author to know.

In May, Poe's story "A Descent into the Maelström" appeared in *Graham's*. In this he returned to the theme of a gigantic whirlpool, which he had used in "MS. Found in a

Bottle" and hinted at in the conclusion of *The Narrative of Arthur Gordon Pym*. The image of a huge mass of turbulent water swirling around and then disappearing down a deep round hole which it had made in itself seems to have fascinated Poe all his life.

In the May issue, he also reviewed two of Dickens' recently published novels, *Master Humphrey's Clock* and *The Old Curiosity Shop*. He paid tribute to the young British writer's work and recognized the fact that Dickens was no ordinary novelist but a genius.

Poe's relations with Graham were so good at this time that the two men made plans to start the *Penn Magazine*. They were going to call upon leading writers like Washington Irving, Henry Wadsworth Longfellow, and William Cullen Bryant for paid contributions. But again Poe was unable to raise enough money to support his share of the venture.

Money was always his big problem. Through a friend, Poe tried to get a clerkship in the Treasury Department. It was a sinecure with a salary of $1000 a year—$200 more than he was earning as editor of *Graham's*. But he did not even have the fare to go from Philadelphia to Washington to apply in person for the position. He would have been glad to get almost any kind of steady Federal appointment, even a $500 one, he said.

During the second half of 1841, Poe was busy writing another article about cryptography. He also did a series of short articles on nearly a hundred American authors, most of them now utterly forgotten. As a journalistic trick, woodcuts of the authors' signatures were used to illustrate each piece.

Since Poe was under the impression that all 750 copies

of *Tales of the Grotesque and Arabesque* had been sold and that there might be some need for a revised edition, he wrote the publishers a letter that is one of the saddest in the annals of American authorship:

Philadelphia, August 13, 1841

Mess. Lea & Blanchard

Gentlemen,   I wish to publish a new collection of my prose Tales with some such title as this—

"*The Prose Tales of Edgar A. Poe, Including "The Murders in the Rue Morgue." The "Descent into the Maelström," and all his later pieces, with a second edition of the "Tales of the Grotesque and Arabesque," "*

The "later pieces" will be eight in number, making the entire collection thirty-three—which would occupy two *thick* novel volumes.

I am anxious that your firm should continue to be my publishers, and, if you would be willing to bring out the book, I should be glad to accept the terms which you allowed me before—that is—you receive all profits, and allow me twenty copies for distribution to friends.

Will you be kind enough to give me an early reply to this letter, and believe me

Yours very resp^t.

Edgar A. Poe

But Lea and Blanchard had lost all interest in Edgar A. Poe. Some copies of the first edition remained unsold, and it was obvious that a publishing firm could not make money out of a writer whose work was so little in demand even when the firm was "to receive all profits." Yet Poe did not give up. He went on preparing a table of contents for a two-volume collection entitled *Phantasy Pieces* which was to contain eleven new stories. Somewhere, sometime, he felt, there would be a publisher who would want his work.

Poe was writing not only for *Graham's* but for others as well. *The Gift*, an illustrated Christmas annual for 1842 but issued late in 1841, had his love story "Eleonora" in it. Autobiographical references are many: Eleonora is obviously Virginia, "a maiden artless and innocent," and the narrator lives with his cousin-wife and her mother. Evidently Poe knew when he wrote "Eleonora" that Virginia was afflicted with tuberculosis, for he says of his heroine: "She had seen that the finger of Death was upon her bosom." In the story, she dies.

Poe had dreaded the possibility that he might go insane. "Eleonora" begins with the statement "Men have called me mad." He goes on to say that "the question is not yet settled, whether madness is or is not the loftiest intelligence—whether all that is profound—does not spring from disease of thought —from *moods* of mind exalted at the expense of the general intellect."

Mad or not, Poe proved to be a first-rate editor for *Graham's Magazine*. On October 27, he said that the circulation, which had been 5000 when first combined with *Burton's*, was increasing so greatly that 25,000 copies were to be printed in January. "Such a thing was never heard of before," he said. But he was still hoping to start the *Penn*. Yet Graham, good as he had been to Poe, was not paying him adequately or even admitting that the magazine's success was due to his creative editorship or to the material he had contributed to it.

Although we have no records about the way the Poes spent the Christmas of 1841, it should have been the happiest one of their lives. He was regularly employed by a magazine that was making money; he had published a number of good things during the year; and his ever-active brain was teeming with ideas. It even looked as if he might soon be able to start his own magazine, perhaps in association with George Graham. And his name was better known, so it was becoming easier for him to sell pieces to other journals.

Mrs. Clemm kept the little household together and managed it very well. Poe was teaching Virginia French. He had bought a harp for her out of his increased earnings, and she played it with delight, singing as she played. They also had a piano. Perhaps she celebrated that forgotten Christmas with some music and songs.

They were living on Coates Street in a small three-story brick house, one of a row of attached, identical buildings with white marble steps leading up to the entrance. Philadelphia and Baltimore had thousands of such dwellings; they were typical of those cities. They were inexpensive to buy or rent, completely undistinguished but practical and comfortable. With them lived Catterina, a big black cat that was Virginia's special pet and close companion.

All went well for about three weeks; then, in the middle of January 1842, misfortune struck again, this time at poor Virginia. She was playing the piano and singing, when she suddenly stopped and choked. Blood ran from her mouth, the dreaded blood that comes from the breaking of a diseased vessel in infected lungs.

It was the beginning of the end, although she was to live

for five more years. But they were dreadful years during which she was never really well. Blood vessels in the lungs broke again a year later, and then, as Poe wrote, "again—again—again and even once again at varying intervals."

Life was never to be the same in the Poe household. Its most beloved member was always near to death, and everyone knew it. Virginia tried to be brave and cheerful, but one had only to look at her to see how the already slight little girl was slowly wasting away.

George Graham later testified to Poe's tender relationship to Virginia:

> His love for his wife was a sort of rapturous worship of the spirit of beauty which he felt was fading before his eyes. I have seen him hovering around her . . . with all the fond fear and tender anxiety of a mother for her first-born—her slightest cough causing in him a shudder, a heart-chill that was visible. . . . It was this hourly *anticipation* of her loss that made him a sad and thoughtful man.

But this was written after Poe's death. Graham was far less sympathetic at the time of Virginia's first seizure. On the day after it, Poe asked for an advance of two months' salary, but Graham refused, and, according to Poe, did so "flatly and discourteously."

Poe was emotionally upset by what was happening to his beloved wife, although the full import of it came only later when she got steadily worse.

In the spring of 1842, Poe was still making plans for his own magazine. He resented his arrangement with Graham, particularly because he had received nothing for his publication's great success. "If, instead of a paltry salary," he wrote, "Graham had given me a tenth of his Magazine, I should feel myself a rich man today."

Because of Virginia's illness, Poe needed money more than ever. Yet he resigned as editor of Graham's with the May 1842 number. He was busy enough and was completing his second detective story, "The Mystery of Marie Rogêt," which is based on the actual murder of a young salesgirl, Mary Rogers, who had been killed near New York City in August 1841. Poe shifted the scene to Paris in order to have the case come to the attention of C. Auguste Dupin.

The story, unfortunately, is slow moving, unnecessarily complicated, inconclusive in its ending, and unduly long. It gives us a further glimpse of the always-fascinating Dupin, but even he is not at his best here. "Marie Rogêt" is a definite comedown from "The Murders in the Rue Morgue." And Poe had trouble selling it to a magazine. It was finally published in three installments in Snowden's Ladies' Companion at the end of 1842.

Poe was now working hard, probably to forget his personal troubles. It was during this period that he wrote one of his finest suspense stories, "The Pit and the Pendulum," a tale of ingenious torture by the Spanish Inquisition. It appeared, oddly enough, in the Christmas annual, The Gift, at the end of 1842. Most of Poe's stories are slow in getting under way, but "The Pit and the Pendulum" has a superb opening, and there is no letdown anywhere.

Poe never gave up trying to get backing for a magazine of his own. One thing he wanted to do in it, he said, was to "make war to the knife against the New England assumption of 'all the decency and all the talent.' " He wanted to feature Southern authors because he believed the Northerners were being unduly favored. The man who had signed his first book "By a Bostonian" had now turned against the section where he had been born.

During the spring of 1842, Dickens stopped in Philadelphia while on his first American visit. The enormously successful British novelist had read Poe's favorable reviews of his work with great interest, and the two men met. Unfortunately, not much is known about what they had to say to each other, but they may very well have discussed the lack of an international copyright law which was hurting them both. In fact, Poe's publisher, Lea and Blanchard, was one of the many who were pirating Dickens' work in America.

This unhappy year in Poe's life was nevertheless enormously productive, and he did some of his most enduring work then. "The Tell-Tale Heart" must have been written during this time, for it was printed in January 1843 in the first issue of James Russell Lowell's short-lived magazine, The Pioneer, which also published Poe's fine poem, "Lenore," in February. "The Tell-Tale Heart" is the most modern of Poe's short stories, a genuine psychological study of murder and conscience that foreshadowed schools of writing yet to come. Not a word is wasted, and the plot drives through to its dramatic climax with a directness that was unusual for its day.

Also written in 1842, although not published until 1843, were two other stories that rank among Poe's best, "The Black Cat" and "The Gold-Bug."

In the sadistic tale, "The Black Cat," Poe introduces

two autobiographical elements: one is the fact that the narrator is heavily addicted to the use of alcohol; the other is the spirit of perverseness which drives men to do senseless, destructive things. In this story he asks the self-revealing question: "Who has not, a hundred times, found himself committing a vile or stupid action, for no other reason than because he knows he should not?" Anyone who wants to understand Poe should remember these words. They clarify many of his otherwise puzzling actions. He returned to the same theme a few years later in "The Imp of the Perverse."

In "The Gold-Bug," Poe showed his interest in deductive reasoning and also in deciphering secret messages. The tale is not really a detective story because it does not present the reader with any evidence until the solution has been given. But it is so close to this kind of tale that anyone who cares about the development of such fiction will want to read it. For the first time, Poe was fairly well paid for writing a story. Graham's bought it for $52 and then released it to Poe so he could enter it in a contest where it won the first prize of $100. It appeared in two installments in the *Dollar Newspaper* late in June 1843 and was reprinted in three parts a few days later in the *Saturday Courier*. It was so popular that the *Dollar Newspaper* had to bring it out again. Then it was made into a short play and produced in Philadelphia.

8

The Ever-Beckoning
Will-of-the-Wisp

‣‣

I hope to issue the first number of "The Stylus,"
a new monthly with some novel features.
—Letter to James Russell Lowell, March 27, 1843

On the last day of January 1843, it looked as if Poe were
really going to have a chance to start his own magazine, for
on that day he signed an agreement to edit a journal that was
to be named *The Stylus*. Meanwhile he hoped to become an
assistant editor on the *Saturday Museum*, but he did not get
the job, although that paper published a long biography of
him with a woodcut portrait. Poe did not like the picture and
said of it: "I am ugly enough, God knows, but not quite so
bad as that." The biography, for which Poe obviously had
supplied the data, was part fact, part fantasy.

This personal account, which was written by a young
lawyer friend of Poe's, gives an excellent description of him:

He is now but a little more than thirty years of age [actu-
ally 34]; in person he is somewhat slender, about five feet,

eight inches in height, and well proportioned; his complexion is rather fair; his eyes are grey and restless, exhibiting a marked nervousness; while the mouth indicates great decision of character; his forehead is extremely broad. . . . His hair is nearly black and partially curling.

It will be noted that Poe did not have a mustache at this time; he grew one later.

Despite the publicity he was getting, Poe was still eager to obtain a government job for its steady income. He had given up hope for an appointment in the Treasury and was now hoping for a place in the Philadelphia Customs Office. He knew that Hawthorne had recently been made an official measurer of salt, coal, and other raw materials in Boston. Since such jobs were given out in Washington, Poe went there in March to make a personal application. What happened is not entirely clear, but the record shows that he got so outrageously drunk on a small amount of port wine that he had to be put on a train and shipped back to Philadelphia. A friend said: "If he took but one glass of weak wine or beer or cider, the Rubicon of the cup was passed, and it almost always ended in excess and sickness. . . . He was one of those temperaments whose only safety is in total abstinence."

The Imp of the Perverse was pushing Poe to the edge again. He had spoiled all chance of getting any kind of government job, and now his two would-be partners in *The Stylus* lost interest. Virginia, perhaps disturbed by her husband's fall from grace again, became seriously ill.

Yet Poe did not give up. In the spring of 1843, he moved his family to pleasanter quarters in the Spring Garden district. And in July, he registered his name in the District Court of

Philadelphia, so he could study law in the office of the friend who had written his biography for the *Saturday Museum*. But he soon abandoned the effort to interest himself in legal affairs.

Getting his work published, however, was of prime importance. He succeeded in persuading a publisher to start a pamphlet series to reprint his stories. In July, the first of *The Prose Romances of Edgar A. Poe* appeared in what was announced as the "Uniform Serial Edition." But that first number was the only one ever printed. As a result, this 12½-cent paperback is now one of the rarest and highest-priced of all Poe's printed works.

By this time, Poe had tired of solving ciphers. Yet in August 1843, he was again tempted to try his hand at one, and, as usual, he succeeded brilliantly. Nevertheless, he said that people were mistaken in supposing that he took pride in his solutions. Then he added: "I feel little pride about anything."

Pressed as always for money, Poe began a new career. On November 21, he gave a lecture on American poetry in Philadelphia and then went on to repeat it in two Delaware cities and also in Baltimore and Reading. He had a good voice, read poetry well, and although one might expect an introvert like Poe to be afraid of an audience, he was not. Mixed in with Poe's diffidence and retiring manner was a streak of aggressiveness. This came out when he got drunk and was the reason for his belligerent behavior when alcohol removed his natural inhibitions.

Since Poe had several stories published in the spring of 1844 he must have written them during the previous winter.

One, "The Spectacles," shows him at his ludicrous worst, for it is about a man who refuses to wear glasses even though his sight is so bad that he does not recognize his own great-great-grandmother and so falls in love with her. Another, "A Tale of the Ragged Mountains," which was published in *Godey's Lady's Book* in April, is far more interesting. In it, Poe uses for his setting the beautiful country near the University of Virginia. Here he displays his growing interest in mesmerism, as hypnotism was then called, and also in the effect of drugs on the mind. In the story a young man in Charlottesville dreams that he goes back to the previous century in India where he becomes involved in a revolt in which he is killed. Then he actually does die in Virginia in much the same way.

Despite all the trouble that Poe had been through during his six years in Philadelphia, he had achieved a great deal there, especially in writing short stories. In April 1844, however, he decided to move back to New York. He and Virginia went on ahead, leaving Mrs. Clemm to sell some of Poe's books and thus raise some money.

In those days, to get from Philadelphia to New York, one had to cross the Delaware River by ferry, take a train across New Jersey to Perth Amboy, and there embark on a steamboat that landed in lower Manhattan. It was raining hard when they arrived, so Poe left Virginia on the boat while he searched the area for a place for them to stay. He soon found a boardinghouse on Greenwich Street near Cedar Street. It was old and "looked buggy," he wrote to Mrs. Clemm, but he got a room and board for two people for $7 a week; "the cheapest board I ever knew," he added.

Since food was a major item in the Poe budget, he described the meals in detail:

For supper, we had the nicest tea you ever drank, strong and hot—wheat bread and rye bread—cheese—tea-cakes (elegant) a great dish (2 dishes) of elegant ham, and 2 of cold veal, piled up like a mountain and large slices—3 dishes of the cakes, and every thing in the greatest profusion. No fear of starving here. The landlady seemed as if she couldn't press us enough, and we were at home directly. For breakfast we had excellent-flavored coffee, hot and strong—not very clear and no great deal of cream—veal cutlets, elegant ham and eggs and nice bread and butter. I never sat down to a more plentiful or a nicer breakfast. I wish you could have seen the eggs— and the great dishes of meat. I ate the first hearty breakfast I have eaten since we left our little home.

He added a postscript to the letter in which he asked Mrs. Clemm to be sure to return a bound volume of the *Southern Literary Messenger* which he had borrowed from a friend. But Mrs. Clemm had sold it along with other books. This caused Poe much embarrassment, especially since he insisted that his mother-in-law must have returned it, only to have it turn up later in a secondhand bookstore.

Poe had just $4.50 left when he settled down in his new quarters. He told Mrs. Clemm that he hoped to borrow $3 more to keep him going for another fortnight. And he also assured her that he hadn't "drank a drop." Liquor was very cheap in those days when there was no tax on alcohol, but one wonders how a man living on the edge of starvation ever had enough money to buy it.

Nine years earlier, in 1835, Poe had published his imaginary account of Hans Pfaall's trip to the moon. Richard Adams

Locke then outdid him with a fictitious tale about life on the moon as seen by telescope, which created a tremendous sensation when it appeared in the New York *Sun*. Now, a few days after Poe arrived in New York for his second attempt to conquer that great publishing center, he sold the editors of the *Sun* another hoax, one about crossing the Atlantic Ocean in a balloon. The trip had supposedly been made in three days from Europe to Sullivan's Island, near Charleston. He described the excitement in New York on April 13 when the story broke:

> The whole square surrounding the *Sun* building was literally besieged. . . . As soon as the first few copies made their way into the streets, they were bought up at almost any price. . . . I saw a half-dollar given . . . for a single paper, and a shilling was a frequent price. I tried in vain, during the whole day, to get possession of a copy.

Before he left Philadelphia, Poe had made a deal with the *Columbia Spy*, a small-town Pennsylvania newspaper, for a series of articles about New York entitled "Doings of Gotham." The description of the Balloon Hoax was quickly reprinted in that paper.

The city he wrote about in "Doings of Gotham" was growing rapidly. Although the built-up section extended only a little way above Union Square, streets had already been mapped out far to the north of that. Poe correctly predicted that before long "every noble cliff will become a pier, and the whole island will be densely desecrated by buildings of brick."

In order to write these articles, he had to explore New

York, which must have been a pleasant task then. Near 84 Street and Broadway, which is now in the heart of a heavily built-up district, he found a 200-acre farm owned by Patrick Brennan. It stretched down to the shores of the Hudson and was far out in the country, but near enough for Poe to travel five miles to the downtown publishing houses when he had to.

The Brennans had never taken boarders, but Poe persuaded them to do so, and his little family—wife, mother-in-law, cat, and all—moved to the farm. It was to be a productive place for writing.

Poe often exchanged letters with James Russell Lowell about literature, publishing, and other subjects of interest to authors. On July 2, 1844, he wrote one that tells us a great deal about his own personality:

My Dear Mr. Lowell,

I can feel for the "constitutional indolence" of which you complain—for it is one of my own besetting sins. I am excessively slothful and wonderfully industrious—by fits. There are epochs when any kind of mental exercise is torture, and when nothing yields me pleasure but solitary communion with the "mountains and the woods,"—the "altars" of Byron. I have thus rambled and dreamed away whole months, and awake, at last, to a sort of mania for composition. Then I scribble all day, and read all night, so long as the disease endures. . . .

I am not ambitious—unless negatively. I now and then feel stirred up to excel a fool, merely because I hate to let a fool imagine that he may excel me. Beyond this I feel nothing of ambition. I really perceive that vanity about which most men merely prate,—the vanity of the human or temporal life. I live continually in a reverie of the future. I have no faith in human perfectibility. I think that human exertion will have no appreciable effect upon humanity. Man is now only more active—not more happy—nor more wise, than he was 6000 years ago. . . .

My life has been whim—impulse—passion—a longing for solitude—a scorn of all things present, in an earnest desire for the future.

Poe expressed some of the ideas voiced in this letter in an article entitled "Mesmeric Revelation," which appeared in the *Columbian Magazine* in August. From this time on, he was becoming more and more interested in philosophical speculation about the meaning of life.

It was probably while on the Brennan farm that he wrote —or at least put the finishing touches to—his finest detective story, "The Purloined Letter." It marks C. Auguste Dupin's last appearance, and he goes out in a blaze of glory, for he solves this famous problem by sheer reasoning. Neither murder nor violence takes place in this tale of Parisian intrigue, but there is more suspense in it than there is in most gorier tales.

Another piece written at this time, and one that is highly typical of Poe, is "The Premature Burial," which was published in the *Dollar Newspaper* late in July 1844. It begins with several true accounts of people who were buried alive and then goes on with a fictional tale about the narrator's undergoing such an experience. Poe makes the incident seem very real. At the end the reader will be amused to discover the clever device he used.

Although he never stopped thinking about death and

everything connected with it, Poe often had less morbid ideas. Late in October 1844, he wrote a long letter to Lowell suggesting that "a dozen of the most active or influential men of letters in this country should unite for the purpose of publishing a Magazine of high character." Each member was to buy a share of stock for $100 and agree to contribute an article every month. He went into detail about possible circulation and cost and said that he thought that such a publication might return a profit of $5000 a year to its twelve shareholders. Nothing came of his suggestion. Nor have any similar proposals for cooperatively owned and operated writers' magazines ever succeeded. Apparently authors care more for doing their own work than they do for organizing outlets to market it. In Poe's case, he undoubtedly thought up the scheme so he could have a magazine to edit.

His restless mind was always at work. He went to great trouble to bring his *Phantasy Pieces*, which now numbered sixty-six, to the attention of Harper's. But they, remembering the difficulties they had had with Poe before, declined to publish the collection.

He did some lecturing and worked on his projected *Critical History of American Literature*, which he never completed. He also began his "Marginalia" late in 1844. This was a series of short pieces or "fillers," some of which were original while others were excerpts from books or articles he had read and thought interesting. They first appeared in the *Democratic Review* for November 1844.

He did some work for Nathaniel P. Willis, who was editing the *Evening Mirror* and the *Weekly Mirror*. Willis said that Poe was "invariably the same sad-mannered, winning, and refined gentleman" he had always known.

Poe's articles for the *Mirror* included several on the compensation that writers received for their work and the harm done by the lack of international copyright. Yet Poe himself was doing better than he had ever done before. Rufus Griswold was including several examples of his work in his forthcoming *Prose Writers of America*, and James Russell Lowell was gathering information for a long biographical article about him. In it, that well-known critic said: "Mr. Poe has that indescribable something which men have agreed to call genius."

And Poe was putting down on paper the haunting lines that were to make him famous. The sinister black raven, which is ordinarily thought of as a symbol of destiny's darker side, was to bring him worldwide acclaim.

9

The Days of "The Raven"

■←◆◆◆◆◆◆◆◆◆◆◆◆◆◆◆◆◆◆◆◆◆◆◆◆◆◆◆◆◆◆◆◆◆◆◆◆◆◆→■

> . . . I betook myself to linking
> Fancy into fancy, thinking what this ominous bird of yore—
> What this grim, ungainly, ghastly, gaunt, and ominous bird of yore
> Meant in croaking "Nevermore."
>
> —"THE RAVEN," 1845

Although it has been said that Poe spent years writing the 108 lines of "The Raven," it seems more likely that he completed all, or almost all, of it in the Brennan house during the winter of 1844–1845. One clue to this is the fact that he had just read and reviewed Elizabeth Barrett's *Drama of Exile and Other Poems*, which contains "Lady Geraldine's Courtship." From this poem, he borrowed the odd stanza structure, echoes and repetitions, and the kind of final refrains used in "The Raven."

One of his biographers reported that Poe said that the poem "had lain for more than *ten years* in his desk unfinished." This is not impossible, as every poet knows, for ideas sometimes have to ripen for a long while before they are ready to be put into final shape. And the fact that "The Raven" is closely associated with his poem, "Lenore," which he had written, published, and revised again and again over a long period of years, indicates that the origins of "The Raven" may go far back in time. But no earlier versions of it are known to exist.

Poe once said that he had originally intended to use an owl instead of a raven for the sinister bird in the poem. But ravens can utter words and owls cannot, so the raven won. Certainly Poe was familiar with ravens. He had seen them in the courtyard of the Tower of London when he was a young boy, and he used to visit a bird store in Philadelphia where there was a tame raven which he watched with fascinated interest. The raven in Dickens' *Barnaby Rudge* may also have inspired him. When he reviewed that novel in 1842, he mentioned the bird and its prophetic croakings.

The most important information we have about the writing of this famous poem is given by Poe himself in the "Philosophy of Composition," which was published a year after "The Raven" first appeared. Even though Poe invented his theories of composition to fit a work that was already completed, his essay does tell us a great deal about the way he wrote verse.

According to him, the poem was deliberately planned beforehand and "the work proceeded, step by step, to its completion with the precision and rigid consequence of a mathematical problem." The length (about a hundred lines), the setting, and the theme were determined by calculation; and even the refrain, he said, had to incorporate "the long o as the most sonorous vowel, in connection with r as the most producible consonant." And the refrain had to be in keeping with the melancholy tone of the poem. With these given factors, "it would have been absolutely impossible to overlook the word 'Nevermore.' In fact, it was the very first which presented itself." The most melancholy topic, he explained, is Death, which is at its most poetic when allied to Beauty. "The most poetical topic in the world" then "is the death of a beautiful woman." And the person who can speak most convincingly about such a tragedy is her bereaved lover.

This is the essence of early Victorian sentimentality, complete with trappings of the grave, deep sighs, and mournful gestures. But Poe was writing in 1844, when the public was eager for such material. He made the raven an international bird and brought his lost Lenore to world attention.

Despite the fact that "The Raven" was so ideally suited to the times, Poe had at least one rejection (by *Graham's Magazine*) before he found a market for the poem. Soon, however, the *American Review* bought it for its February 1845 number. There the poem was signed "——— Quarles." Even before the *Review* appeared on the stands, Nathaniel P. Willis, who was a versifier of some note himself, read the poem, admired it, and offered to print it in the *New-York Evening Mirror*, which he was editing. It was published there, under Poe's name, in the January 29 issue. Willis wrote an introduction which was sure to attract readers:

> In our opinion, it is the most effective single example of "fugitive poetry" ever published in this country; and unsurpassed in English poetry for subtle conception, masterly ingenuity of versification, and consistent sustaining of imaginative lift and "pokerishness". . . . It will stick to the memory of everyone who reads it.

Willis was certainly right about his last statement. His choice of words, however, needs explanation. "Pokerishness" means something that is mysterious or uncanny. And his use of the term "fugitive poetry" is hardly complimentary to Poe, for this refers to verse that is written for the day and that is thought unlikely to last. Willis was wrong, for "The Raven," even though it is overburdened with Victorian ornament, has lasted very well and is remembered by millions of people who are not familiar with anything else Poe wrote.

"The Raven" also appeared in the New York Tribune for February 4; in the Broadway Journal for February 8; in March in the Southern Literary Messenger; and then it reached London, where it was printed in the Critic on June 14. Before long it was picked up by many other newspapers and magazines.

"The Raven" readily lends itself to parody, and more than a dozen semicomic versions were printed in Poe's lifetime. Most of them had other birds or animals as key figures, although some went farther from the original than this. One that appeared almost immediately was entitled "The Craven" by "Poh" and was an advertisement for medicated soap. Since then scores—and perhaps hundreds—of parodies of "The Raven" have been written, and it is likely that still more will be composed in the future.

The American Review seems to have paid Poe $10 or $15 for the poem, and Willis' Mirror may have contributed a few dollars more. The other papers, which quickly copied "The Raven," probably paid nothing at all for it.

Yet the poem, coming out at the same time that Lowell's favorable biographical article appeared in Graham's, helped to make Poe's name much better known. And that was an enormous aid in selling other writings to publishers.

Aside from the lack of compensation, the fame of "The Raven" did a great deal for Poe. In a letter to a friend, he said that it "has had a great 'run,'—but I wrote it for the express purpose of running—just as I did the 'Gold-Bug'. . . . The bird beat the bug though, all hollow."

Beginning in January 1845, a new weekly publication, the *Broadway Journal*, had appeared on the stands. Poe's long review of Elizabeth Barrett's *Drama of Exile*, with its poem that had given him ideas for the stanza structure of "The Raven," was printed in the first two numbers.

The January 23 issue of the *New-York Evening Mirror* had a short, unsigned poem which has been ascribed to Poe. If it is his, it shows him in a light, jesting mood.

EPIGRAM FOR WALL STREET

I'll tell you a plan for gaining wealth,
  Better than banking, trade or leases—
Take a bank note and fold it up,
  And then you will find your money in *creases!*
This wonderful plan, without danger or loss,
Keeps your cash in your hands, where nothing can trouble it;
And every time you fold it across,
  'Tis as plain as the light of the day that you *double* it!

Poe may have wanted this to appear without his name because he was losing interest in the *Mirror* as an outlet for his work and now preferred the *Broadway Journal*. Evidently its two owners liked what he was doing for them, for on February 22 they printed a notice that he would be "associated with the editorial department." His name was to be on the masthead, and he was to be given a third of the profits the *Journal* hoped to make. This sounds fine, but the major owner told a friend that "Poe is only an assistant to me and will in no way interfere with my own way of doing things."

Poe's contract required him to supply at least a full page of copy every week and also to oversee the general preparation of the paper. One way he managed to fill up space was to reprint some of his stories and poems that had already appeared elsewhere.

Less than a week after he started to work with the *Broadway Journal*, Poe gave a lecture at the New York Society Library, where he praised the verse written by 34-year-old Frances Sargent Osgood. Mrs. Osgood was not present, but she soon heard what Poe had said. She arranged to meet him, and they were formally introduced to each other. Mrs. Osgood was to play an important part in his life, along with other women who now began to show a sudden interest in the hitherto obscure writer who was becoming famous.

Mrs. Osgood had recently quarreled with her husband, a portrait painter to whom she had been married for ten years, and she was therefore in a mood to welcome Poe's attentions. They were entirely platonic, however, and she became good friends with Virginia, who felt that her distinguished husband needed companionship with intellectual women. Mrs. Osgood later wrote one of the best descriptions we have of Poe at work.

> At his desk . . . he would sit, hour after hour, patient, assiduous, and uncomplaining, tracing, in an exquisitely clear chirography and with almost superhuman swiftness, the light-

ning thoughts—with "rare and radiant" fancies as they flashed through his wonderful and ever wakeful brain.

She went on to say that Poe always prepared his longer pieces for the press by pasting the ends of the pages together to make a long narrow roll. In this way he was assured that no separate sheets would be left out and that the printer would have a consecutive run of copy to set in type.

In May, Poe and James Russell Lowell met for the first and only time. Many years later, Lowell wrote a description of his reaction to the man with whom he had often corresponded:

> He was small; his complexion of what I should call a clammy-white; fine, dark eyes, and fine head, very broad at the temples, but receding sharply from the brows backwards. His manner was rather formal, even pompous, but I have the impression he was a little soggy with drink—not tipsy—but as if he had been holding his head under a pump to cool it.

Mrs. Clemm, who was present at the meeting, confirmed the fact that Poe had been drunk then. In a letter to Lowell, written after Poe's death, she said, "The day you saw him in New York *he was not himself.* Do you not remember that I never left the room?"

Early in 1845 the Poes left the Brennan house on 84 Street and moved downtown to stay for a while at 85 Amity Street. Then they went to a boardinghouse on East Broadway. The new location was only seven blocks from the East River, where ships tied up at the many wharves and docks to unload cargoes from ports all over the world. Poe could walk downtown to the publishing center around City Hall.

The *Broadway Journal* was not doing well, and one of its owners bowed out. The July 12 issue announced that Poe would thereafter be in complete charge of the editorial department. This, of course, meant even more work. He continued to reprint his own stories and poems. In this way they came to the attention of publishers, and Wiley and Putnam agreed to bring out a collection of twelve of his stories under the modest title *Tales*. The book sold for 50 cents, out of which he was to receive a royalty of eight cents a copy. Poe did not have the right to choose the stories, so the little volume contained at least four that are far from his best. But all the detective stories were in it, and so were "The Black Cat," "The Gold-Bug," and "The Fall of the House of Usher."

During the year 1845, Poe had six new stories published. Only one of them—"The Facts in the Case of M. Valdemar" —is of any interest, and that, because of its graphic description of the sudden decay of a corpse preserved for six months by hypnosis, is so likely to repel readers that it is seldom included in any modern collection of Poe's work.

Even though he was now editor of the *Broadway Journal*, Poe still hoped to have his own magazine and said so in a letter to his cousin Neilson Poe in Baltimore. Living on East Broadway had not turned out well, and the family returned to 85 Amity Street before the end of the year.

In that location, now Third Street, one block south of Washington Square, Poe was in the center of New York's cultural life. Since he was making a name for himself, he was in demand at parties. Sometimes he was called upon to recite not only "The Raven" but other of his lesser known works. He was now at the top of his career, editor of the *Broadway Journal*, and author of the collected *Tales*, which was attracting enough purchasers to make its publishers think that a volume of his poetry might have a ready market. They signed a contract to bring out *The Raven and Other Poems* and had it in the bookstores before the year was over.

Poe was allowed to choose the poems he wanted to appear in the volume. He picked twenty for the 31-cent paperbound book and still further revised some of them. He dedicated the collection to Elizabeth Barrett, who was soon to marry Robert Browning. When she wrote to thank Poe, she told him that "The Facts in the Case of M. Valdemar" was being widely reprinted—without payment, of course—in British newspapers. It was also brought out in London in pamphlet form.

One day, late in the autumn of 1845, a writer ten years younger than Poe dropped into the office of the *Broadway Journal*. There is no record of what the two authors discussed that day, but the visitor, whose name was Walt Whitman, had sent the *Journal* an article entitled "Art Singing and Heart Singing." Poe published it on November 29. Whitman was almost unknown at this time, although he had written a very bad novel, *Franklin Evans*, in 1842. Oddly enough, it was a tale about a young man who was addicted to alcohol and who suffered terrible degradations from it until he reformed.

Although Poe wrote in a letter sent to a friend in August that he had stopped drinking and had "resolved not to touch a drop" as long as he lived, he was unable to keep his resolution for any length of time. Through Lowell, he was invited to lecture in Boston for a fee of $50, and there he got into trouble again.

He was preceded at the Lyceum by a political speaker

who went on and on until the audience was too restless to appreciate anyone's poetry. Poe made the mistake of reading his long philosophical poem, "Al Aaraaf," and lost many of his listeners. A reading of "The Raven," however, held those who were left. Then he made the further mistake of drinking champagne with the other speaker and some of the dignitaries who had been at the lecture. The wine had a quick effect on him. While under its influence, he damned Boston and said he was ashamed of the fact that he had been born there.

Boston papers reviewed the lecture unfavorably, and an editorial in the important *Transcript* called his performance a failure. Poe promptly replied by publishing a long account of the evening in the *Broadway Journal*. No one came out of the affair well, but Poe did worst of all.

There is more to the Boston story than appears on the surface. Poe was under great tension at this time, for the *Journal* was doing so badly that he was soon given complete control and ownership of the paper for a few dollars plus taking over its debts. For this, he had to raise money, greater sums than he had ever needed before. He wrote desperate letters to friends, authors, and publishers, and succeeded in getting nearly enough money to put him in the clear. But it was not enough. Matters got steadily worse.

For two months during the late autumn of 1845, he was so sick and depressed that at one time he believed that he was going mad. In order to get the paper out, he had to do all the writing and editing himself and handle all the business affairs besides.

Then, on top of everything else, Virginia became seriously ill again. Poe decided to give up office work and go to the country for six months or a year to restore his health and spirits.

On January 3, 1846, a notice appeared in the *Journal* saying that its editor was bidding farewell—"as cordially to foes as to friends."

10

A Cottage in the Bronx

Give me a cottage for my home
And a rich old cypress vine.

—VIRGINIA POE, 1846

The year 1845, which had begun so auspiciously for Poe, with wide acclaim for "The Raven" and what seemed to be the beginning of a new career as editor of the Broadway Journal, ended in the worst disaster of his life. And he was haunted by fear of madness.

Eager as the Poes were to move to the country, they remained in the Amity Street house for some time. They may also have returned for a short while to the Brennan farm, where "The Raven" had been written. Then they stayed briefly in a house at the eastern end of 47 Street in the Turtle Bay section. There Poe used to row out to visit some of the islands in the East River.

Virginia, just as much as Poe himself, wanted to live in the country. A valentine she wrote for her husband shows

that. It may seem naïve, but it is more artful than it appears
to be, for it is an acrostic with the first letter of each line
spelling out his name:

> Ever with thee I wish to roam—
> Dearest my life is thine.
> Give me a cottage for my home
> And a rich old cypress vine,
> Removed from the world with its sin and care
> And the tattling of many tongues.
> Love alone shall guide us when we are there—
> Love shall heal my weakened lungs;
> And Oh, the tranquil hours we'll spend,
> Never wishing that others may see!
> Perfect ease we'll enjoy, without thinking to lend
> Ourselves to the world and its glee—
> Ever peaceful and blissful we'll be.
>
> Saturday, February 14, 1846

It took time for Poe to find the sort of place they both
wanted, but by late spring he had located what seemed to be
an ideal home for them. It was a small cottage surrounded by
an acre of ground with lilac bushes and cherry trees growing
near the house. The first floor had a living room, a tiny bed-
room for Virginia, and an extension that was the kitchen.
There was also a low-ceilinged attic with two unheated rooms
in which the only ventilation was supplied by squat little
windows. The cottage was in Fordham, thirteen miles from
New York, but it could be reached by train. The rent was
$100 a year.

The building, which originally stood on the east side of
Kingsbridge Road near what is now 192 Street, was moved

a few hundred feet north in 1913 and is near Poe Park, where it can be visited. The city is all around it now with built-up areas stretching away in every direction, but the West Farms area was pleasantly rural then. Today, having a cottage in the Bronx may not sound very attractive, but the Bronx at that time was very different.

Poe seldom left Virginia alone there (actually she was never alone, for her mother was with her), but on June 15, 1846, when he unexpectedly had to stay overnight in New York, he wrote a letter to assure her of his love:

> My Dear Heart, My Dear Virginia!
>
> In my last great disappointment, I should have lost my courage *but for you*—my darling little wife, you are my greatest and *only* stimulus now to battle with this uncongenial, unsatisfactory, and ungrateful life. . . . Until I see you, I will keep in *loving remembrance* your *last words* and your fervant [*sic*] prayer!
>
> Sleep well and may God grant you a peaceful summer, with your devoted
>
> Edgar

Except for the brief note to Virginia written at the end of a message to Mrs. Clemm in 1835, this is the only letter we have that Poe wrote to his wife. He must have sent her many, however, for he said in a letter to a friend that when he was away she would fret if "she did not hear from me twice a day."

The little cottage was far from the busy city, but visitors came to see the Poes. Most of them were friends, but one was a spiteful woman whose chief aim in life seemed to be to stir up trouble. She was Mrs. E. F. Ellet, a poetess whose work

Poe had reviewed. For some reason she imagined that Mrs. Osgood, who was devoted to Virginia, was in love with Poe. With Puritanical zeal, she sent two women to the Fordham cottage to demand that Poe return Mrs. Osgood's letters. He did so, but was terribly disturbed by the unpleasant incident. Mrs. Ellet was to reappear later in his life. Writing about her then, he called her a fiend and warned others to beware of her.

As usual, Poe sought refuge from his misery by working hard at his writing. He was doing a series of articles for *Godey's* on "The Literati of New York City," and was striking out with malice at authors he particularly disliked. What he had to say about Thomas Dunn English angered that writer so much that he launched into a violent counterattack on Poe, which the *New-York Evening Mirror* printed. The two men had known each other in Philadelphia where Poe had harshly criticized a book of English's poems. He also claimed that he had at one time given English "a flogging which he will remember to the day of his death—and, luckily, in the presence of witnesses." Since English was a big man and Poe a small one, not noted for his physical prowess, this seems questionable. The quarrel, however, was on, and it became increasingly bitter. Poe's criticisms of English were often unfair and sometimes inconsistent, for at one time he said, "I do not personally know Mr. English."

In his article in the *Mirror*, English was not only violent but went so far as to assert that Poe was guilty of forgery. This was quickly disproved, but English was incautious enough to write to the *Mirror*, challenging Poe to bring suit. This Poe promptly did and won $225 as damages plus costs. For a moment it seemed as though litigation paid better than literature, but as a result of the case Poe had his series on the Literati cancelled and his drinking habits aired publicly in court.

The stopping of the Literati articles was unfortunate because they were to be part of a book to be entitled *Literary America, Some Honest Opinions about our Autorial Merits and Demerits with Occasional Words of Personality.* Part of this exists in manuscript, but it has never been published.

Poe's anger at this unfortunate affair may have worked itself off in the writing of one of his very best stories, "The Cask of Amontillado" (1846), a tale of revenge that takes place in Italy. Here Poe shows how sparse with words he can be; the story marches with deadly intent to its carefully planned ending.

Mrs. Mary Gove, an advocate of health reform and one of the Literati, gives us a description of the way the Poes lived during the summer of 1846: "There was a piazza in front of the house that was a lovely place to sit . . . with the shade of cherry trees before it. There was no cultivation, no flowers— nothing but the smooth greensward and the majestic trees."

As to the house itself: "The floor of the kitchen was as white as wheaten flour. A table, a chair, and a little stove . . . seemed to furnish it perfectly. The sitting-room floor was laid with a check matting; four chairs, a light stand, and a hanging bookshelf completed its furniture. There were pretty presentation copies of books . . . and the Brownings had posts of honor."

As to the people who lived in the cottage: "The mother [Mrs. Clemm], then more than sixty years of age . . . was a tall, dignified old lady, with a most ladylike manner, and her black dress, though old and much worn, looked really elegant on her. She wore a widow's cap . . . and it suited exquisitely with her snow-white hair. . . . Mrs. Poe looked very young; she had large black eyes, and a pearly whiteness of complexion, which was a perfect pallor. Her pale face, her brilliant eyes, and her raven hair gave her an unearthly look. . . . When she coughed it was made certain that she was rapidly passing away."

One afternoon the male visitors were playing games, which required them to leap high into the air. This brought about a minor disaster for Poe. When he landed, he split his one and only pair of shoes so badly that they were damaged beyond repair. The woebegone look on his face as he examined the gaping rips touched some of the guests, but there was nothing they could do.

Mrs. Clemm had an immediate solution. Among the visitors was an editor who had been holding one of Poe's manuscripts for more than a week while he made up his mind about publishing it. Mrs. Clemm took one of the ladies aside and asked her to try to persuade the editor to buy it on the spot. Then, she said, "Eddie can have a new pair of shoes."

The woman did so; the manuscript was bought and paid for; and Poe presumably got the shoes he so badly needed.

Discussion of the manuscript in question had already taken place at the outdoor party, and the fact that those who had seen it said that they "could not make head or tail out of it" has led some biographers to believe that it was an early draft of the famous but difficult poem "Ulalume." Recent discoveries, however, indicate that the manuscript which was to pay for Eddie's new shoes was "The Rationale of Verse," a very personal analysis of the theories of English versification.

Poe was so ill during most of 1846 that he was unable to do much writing. His quarrel and lawsuit with English, the obvious decline of Virginia's health, and a constant lack of money all added to his difficulties. "I feel ill, and am ground into the very dust with poverty," he wrote in a letter to a friend that summer. But he never gave up hoping to start his own literary magazine, and he undoubtedly still wanted to have an up-to-date and more complete collection of his works published. He was not to have that privilege, however.

Meanwhile, Poe was becoming skeptical about the value of some of his own work, particularly his detective stories. On August 9, 1846, he said in a letter:

> You are right about the hair-splitting of my French friend (Dupin):—that it is all done for effect. These tales of ratiocination owe most of their popularity to being something in a new key. I do not mean to say that they are not ingenious—but people think them more ingenious than they are—on account of their method and *air* of method. In the "Murders in the Rue Morgue," for instance, where is the ingenuity of unravelling a web which you yourself (the author) have woven for the express purpose of unravelling? The reader is made to confound the ingenuity of the supposititious Dupin with that of the writer of the story.

As winter came on, Virginia got steadily worse. Mrs. Gove visited the cottage again and reported:

> There was no clothing on the bed, which was only straw, but a snow-white spread and sheets. The weather was cold,

and the sick lady had the dreadful chills that accompany the hectic fevers of consumption. She lay on the straw bed, wrapped in her husband's great-coat, with a large tortoise-shell cat on her bosom. The wonderful cat seemed conscious of her great usefulness. The coat and the cat were the sufferer's only means of warmth, except as her husband held her hands, and her mother her feet.

Mrs. Gove enlisted the aid of Mrs. Marie Louise Shew in the cause of the dying girl. She was the only daughter of a doctor and had had some medical training. Although she lived in Greenwich Village, she traveled every other day to Fordham to look after Virginia. The first thing she did was to bring enough bedclothes to keep the patient warm. Then she raised $60 by appealing to her friends for help. Poe was so appreciative that he later addressed three poems to her.

Some items about the plight of the Poes appeared in New York and Philadelphia papers, and Nathaniel P. Willis, who had always been helpful, wrote a long editorial in the *Home Journal* about the crisis in the family. He said that in the past, Poe had always "been deeply mortified and distressed by the discovery that his friends had been called upon for assistance." Under the circumstances, however, Willis said he had "little doubt that a generous gift could hardly be better applied to than to him," and he offered to forward any money that might be sent in as a "tribute of sympathy with genius."

Poe was unhappy about attention being drawn to his predicament. He wrote to Willis, saying that it was true that his wife was ill and that he was also and that they were in want of money, but they certainly had many friends to whom he could have applied for aid. He ended the letter: "The truth is, I have a great deal to do; and I have made up my mind not to die till it is done."

The question, however, was not his illness or possible death, but Virginia's. During the cold month of January her health kept failing until it was obvious that she had not long to live. She gave some of her things to Mrs. Shew and sank slowly, day after day.

On January 29, Poe wrote to Mrs. Shew to convey Virginia's farewell to her and thank her for all that she had done. Both Poe and Virginia begged her to come to Fordham the next day.

But on that next day Virginia was dead. After her funeral Poe wrote a brief poem to commemorate her passing:

> Deep in earth my love is lying,
> And I must weep alone.

11

To Helen – and Others

■◆◆■

I saw that you were my *Helen*—my Helen—
the Helen of a thousand dreams.

—LETTER TO MRS. SARAH HELEN WHITMAN, October 1, 1848

One might think that so sensitive a man as Poe would write poems about his dead wife, but he did not. He took her death badly and often visited her grave and came home weeping.

Mrs. Clemm and Mrs. Shew took turns in caring for him. Because of her medical background, Mrs. Shew thought she could supply data for a diagnosis of what was physically wrong with Poe. She consulted Dr. Valentine Mott of the School of Medicine of New York University and told the doctor that Poe had an intermittent pulse with a long pause after ten regular heartbeats. She believed that he had a lesion on one side of the brain. His twisted face, with two very different halves, might confirm this. But amateur diagnosis, made more than a century ago, is hardly reliable. From this time on, Poe needed a psychiatrist more than a medical doctor. The insanity he had always dreaded was creeping up on him, and his bouts with liquor became worse as his misery increased.

There was very little creative ability left in him so far as prose was concerned, but he was still able to write some truly memorable poetry. This was when he wrote "Ulalume," but no matter what name the dead or dying woman bears— Lenore, Eleonora, Morella, Ligeia, or Annabel Lee—she is always the same symbol of departed youth and beauty, the victim of an early death.

American newspapers and their editors were harshly outspoken in the 1840's, and even during this sad time, they did not leave Poe in peace. The *Saturday Evening Post* charged him with having committed plagiarism in *The Conchologist's First Book*, which he had compiled eight years before. He was angered by the accusation and threatened to bring suit, but someone persuaded him not to do so. He also got into a wrangle with the powerful New York journalist, Horace Greeley of the *Tribune*, over a loan of $50 which Greeley had advanced him in 1845 to help him purchase the *Broadway Journal*. But the *Journal* had gone under, and Poe was now in no position to pay anyone. Greeley never did get his money, although Poe kept trying to raise funds to pay the debt.

During the summer of 1847, he went to Washington, Alexandria, Baltimore, and Philadelphia to call on magazine editors and owners in some of those cities. Again he was ill, and he may have become so, as he so often did, by indulging in the liquor that had such a powerful effect on him. One man who knew him reported that after Virginia's death Poe did not seem to care whether he lived for a year or a day.

He wanted somehow to replace her, for he felt a desperate need for a woman who would take care of him and love him. He went to Albany, where he called on Mrs. Frances Osgood, whom he had met in New York early in 1845. Her brother-in-law, whose home she was visiting, reported that Poe wanted her to elope with him. He behaved badly during his brief stay in Albany. He also saw Sarah Anna Lewis, a Brooklyn poetess who was married to a lawyer whom Poe knew.

Except for "Ulalume," the year 1847 was understandably unproductive. Poe was thinking of other things now, although he still had not given up hope of having his own magazine. To further it, he meant to go on a lecture tour of the South and the West to get subscribers. Meanwhile, he was concentrating on a subject that had long obsessed him—the nature of the Universe. Indications of his growing interest in cosmology had appeared in his writings for some years. Since publishers did not want his opinions on this vast topic, he had to express his ideas in minor pieces. He first displayed his interest in astronomy in "Al Aaraaf" in 1829, and then again in "The Conversations of Eiros and Charmion" in 1839, and in "The Colloquy of Monos and Una" in 1841. Bits and pieces appeared in "Marginalia," the short fillers he wrote for magazines. Now that Virginia was dead and he was very much alone, he started to put his concepts on paper. Before long, the pages grew into a book-length manuscript.

He had enough written by February 3, 1848, to use the material as the basis for a two-hour lecture entitled "The Universe," which he gave at the New York Society Library. The newspapers praised the speech, but Poe said that they did not understand it. In order to clarify what he meant, he outlined his thesis in a letter to a friend:

The General Proposition is this—Because Nothing was, *therefore* All Things are.

1—An inspection of the *universality of Gravitation*—i.e., of the fact that each particle tends, *not* to any one common point, but to *every other* particle—suggests *perfect* totality or *absolute* unity, as the source of the phenomenon.

2—Gravity is but the mode in which is manifested the tendency of all things to return into their original unity—is but the reaction of the first Divine Act.

3—The *law* regulating the return—i.e., the *law* of Gravitation—is but a necessary result of the necessary and sole possible mode of equable *irradiation* of matter through space: this *equable* irradiation is necessary as a basis for the Nebular Theory of Laplace.

4—The Universe of Stars (contradistinguished from the Universe of Space) is limited.

5—Mind is cognizant of Matter *only* through its two properties, attraction and repulsion: therefore Matter is only attraction and repulsion: a finally consolidated globe-of-globes, being but one particle, would be without attraction—i.e., gravitation: the existence of such a globe presupposed the expulsion of the separative ether which we know to exist between the particles as at present diffused: thus the final globe would be matter without attraction and repulsion: but these *are* matter: then the final globe would be matter without matter—i.e., no matter at all: it must disappear. This Unity is *Nothingness.*

6—Matter springing from Unity, sprang from Nothingness—i.e., was created.

7—All will return to Nothingness, in returning to Unity.

The lecture was a summary of his book, *Eureka,* which was soon accepted for publication by Putnam's, who gave Poe an advance of $14. Even this trivial sum had to be repaid if sales did not cover expenses.

When 750 copies of the book were issued early in July 1848, few people—and even fewer critics—paid any attention to it. The text was difficult to read, and it required a good background in science, particularly in astronomy and physics, as well as some training in theology, to understand the author's erudite references. The book has always been thought of as one of Poe's aberrations and has never been taken seriously. But it cannot be thrust aside, for it represents aspects of him that are important for an understanding of his complex and inventive mind.

He had many interests—science, logic, philosophy, and religion among them. Some of these interests were put to use in his detective stories, in his solution of cryptograms, and in his article on Maelzel's Chess-Player. They also crop up here and there in book reviews and fillers. He is too often thought of only as a writer of horror tales and of romantic elegiac verse. But he was more than that, for he had a superb rational and original mind, perhaps one of the best in the America of his time. He once said that he wondered "what would be the fate of any individual gifted, or rather accursed, with an intellect very far superior to that of his race. Of course, he would be conscious of his superiority; nor could he (if otherwise constituted as man is) help manifesting his consciousness. Thus he would make enemies at all points. And since his opinions and speculations would differ widely from those of all mankind—that he would be considered a madman is evident. . . . Hell could invent no greater torture than that of being charged with abnormal weakness on account of being abnormally strong."

Whether Poe was actually as brilliant as he thought he was does not matter. He considered himself to be far superior to everyone around him. Such an attitude can be a symptom of insanity. It is also just possible that he actually was the greatest intellect in the United States in the 1840's. Certainly he did not have much competition. Leaders of the past, men like Jefferson, were dead, and the great men of nineteenth-century America had not yet proved themselves. Emerson had not yet done his best work; neither had Hawthorne. Thoreau, Melville, and Whitman were still unknown. Even Lincoln was then an obscure Congressman serving his first and only term in the House of Representatives in Washington. The 1840's lack memorable men and deeds. The country was busy with mechanical things, such as railroads, telegraphs, and factories. Meanwhile, the intellect and the arts languished. In such an age, Poe had reason to believe that he was vastly superior to the creatures he saw around him, and they naturally refused to admit that he was.

Today no one is likely to read *Eureka* except as a scholarly chore. Its science is outmoded, as is most scientific writing of that period; its philosophy is hardly original; and its theology does not appeal to the modern mind. But these facts do not matter; the questions to ask are: Is *Eureka* a logical, even though highly individual, explanation of the nature of the universe as one intelligent person saw it in the 1840's? Or is it the ravings of a man who was going mad?

These questions have been put to modern scientists, who agree that *Eureka* is not the work of a disordered mind. In fact, one of them says: "Its author had a keen intelligence and great ability in putting forward his ideas. One must admit the full mental vigor of its author without necessarily agreeing with his conclusions."

The book must be taken for what Poe intended it to be. It was not a scientific treatise; it is clearly defined on its title page: *Eureka, a Prose Poem*. And as such it should be judged.

Eureka was written at a very depressed period in Poe's life. In February 1848 he told a friend that he was now "rigorously abstemious . . . and the causes which maddened me to the drinking point are no more, and I am done drinking forever," but this was only one of the many times he said that.

As an escape from the isolation of the cottage in Fordham, where he had only Mrs. Clemm to talk to, he began to seek the company—and love—of other women. Soon after Virginia's death he wrote an ingenious sonnet to Mrs. Sarah Anna Lewis, the Brooklyn poetess. This short poem, although mediocre, is cleverly done, for her name is concealed in it, not in the initial letters of each line, as in a simple acrostic, but in a more complicated way. The reader must pick out the first letter of the first line, then the second letter of the second line, and so on, going one letter more to the right for each line until her name is spelled out. Poe must have begun by noticing that there were just fourteen letters in the name Sarah Anna Lewis—exactly the right number for a sonnet. His interest in the lady was not merely personal, for her husband had given him $100 to serve as her editor, critic, mentor, publicity agent, and promoter.

He also paid attention to Mrs. Shew, who had been so helpful during Virginia's last hours. He was visiting her in her brother-in-law's home in downtown New York in the spring of 1848 when the bells in the neighborhood all began to ring at once. Poe, who was tired, was rather annoyed by them, but his hostess began to write several lines of verse about the various sounds the bells were making. She even headed the sheet "The Bells, by E. A. Poe." Before long, Poe took the pen from her and revised and expanded what she had put down until he had a short poem. Then he crossed out his name and wrote in hers instead.

He must have had a good opinion of what he had done, for he revised and expanded the poem slightly, and sold it to Sartain's *Union Magazine* for $15. Before it was published, he added more stanzas until it was 112 lines long—four more than "The Raven" had.

"The Bells" is one of the most successful efforts ever made to represent actual sounds in language. It is an outstanding example of onomatopoeia. In it, the vowel sounds are especially important, but so are such consonants as *t, r, n, b,* and *cl*. The poem is most effective when read aloud.

Poe was never to see "The Bells" in print because Sartain was so slow in publishing it that it did not appear in his lifetime.

During 1848, Poe achieved the dubious distinction, along with a score of other noted American authors, of being satirized in James Russell Lowell's *A Fable for Critics*. In that series of profiles written in verse, Lowell said:

> Here comes Poe with his Raven like Barnaby Rudge,
> Three-fifths of him genius and two-fifths sheer fudge.

Poe went to Lowell, Massachusetts, to lecture on poetry on July 10, and while there, met Mrs. Charles B. Richmond, whose given name was Nancy. He preferred to call her Annie and wrote a poem entitled "For Annie." She was an attractive, young married woman, with whom his relations were always platonic even though the language in the letters and poems he addressed to her was not.

Soon after the visit to Lowell, Poe went on his subscriber-seeking tour, starting in Richmond and then going on to Baltimore and Philadelphia. He seems to have behaved fairly well on this trip, although one person said that he had been horribly drunk.

After Poe's return to Fordham, he renewed a correspondence which had begun on St. Valentine's Day when a poem entitled "To Edgar A. Poe" had been read aloud at a party in New York. Since the poem bore the postmark "Providence, Rhode Island," it was easy to guess that it had been written by Sarah Helen Whitman, a fairly well-known versifier who lived in that city. She was a widow, six years older than Poe. Early in June he sent her a poem written in blank verse entitled "To Helen." It is a good piece of romantic verse but a great comedown from the earlier "To Helen" of the 1830's.

On September 21, Poe went to Providence to call on Mrs. Whitman. When he was in that city in the summer of 1845, he had seen her briefly, standing in the garden near her house, dressed all in white. Since they had never really met, he now took with him a letter of introduction. To make sure she would be in Providence when he got there, he sent her a note asking for her autograph. But he signed the note Edward S. T. Grey, again taking refuge behind an assumed name.

Now begins one of the most tangled and overwrought emotional incidents in Poe's tense and complicated life. Mrs. Whitman was a simple woman, genuinely interested in literature and the arts, but she was also a spiritualist who lived with her aged mother and an eccentric sister. She had many friends in literary circles, and people generally tended to be protective of her. She disapproved of drinking but indulged in heavy inhalations of ether, a practice that was then fashionable. In her case, breathing ether was particularly dangerous, for she had some kind of nervous disorder, which Poe thought might be a symptom of heart disease.

Poe felt strongly drawn to this middle-aged woman who had many peculiarities. She had no great fortune or special influence, so he could not be accused of seeking financial gain. The attraction she had for him remains a mystery as do many things in Poe's life.

His lengthy correspondence with Sarah Helen Whitman reviews almost every moment he spent with her. His letters were all protestations of love—and they go on and on about it until they become unconvincing. Even Mrs. Whitman seems to have had her doubts about them.

12

"Good Night, Ladies; Good Night"

■◆◆■

Ah, dream too bright to last!
—"To One in Paradise," 1833–1849

Mrs. Whitman had already been warned about Poe by Mrs. Osgood, who had known him since early 1845. She said: "May Providence protect you. . . . He is in truth, 'A glorious devil, with large heart and brain.'"

A warning phrased in those terms would hardly deter the romantic Mrs. Whitman from wanting to meet so glamorous and noted a figure. They saw each other several times—once, appropriately enough, in a local cemetery.

During one of these meetings, he told her that she was his Helen, his "Helen of a thousand dreams." He also said that he loved her so much that even if she should die, he would willingly—even joyfully—go down with her "into the night of the Grave." Somewhere in the midst of all his ardent declarations of love, he asked her to marry him. She put off giving him an answer, and he returned to Fordham to await her reply.

Instead of a definite answer, a letter came from her which showed that her women friends had been buzzing around. He was accused, among other things, of having "no principle— no moral sense." In his reply, he defended what he called his "Quixotic sense of the honorable—of the chivalrous," and then breached that code by saying untruthfully that he had deliberately renounced John Allan's fortune "rather than endure a trivial wrong." Then, even more reprehensibly, he said that he had married Virginia for her sake, knowing that there was no possibility of his being happy with her.

Poe was at his worst in his relationship with Mrs. Whitman, but he had reached a stage where he was no longer responsible for his actions. When he went to Lowell to lecture again, he stopped off on the way to ask her for an answer about marrying him. She promised to send her reply to Lowell, where he was staying with the Richmonds. When he finally received it, he found that she could still not make up her mind. While he was with the Richmonds, Poe was sure that it was really Annie whom he loved. He was in a bad way, as his letter to her, recounting what happened after he left Lowell, shows:

> I remember nothing distinctly . . . until I found myself in Providence. I went to bed and wept through a long, long, hideous night of despair . . . . Finally, I procured two ounces of laudnum [sic] . . . and took the cars back to Boston. When I arrived, I wrote you a letter in which I opened my whole heart to you—to you—my Annie, whom I so madly, so distractedly love. . . . I then reminded you of that holy promise

... That ... you would come to me on my bed of death. I implore you to come *then*, mentioning the place where I should be found in Boston. Having written this letter, I swallowed about half the laudnum [sic] and hurried to the Post Office. ... But I had not calculated on the strength of the laudanum, for, before I reached the Post Office my reason was entirely gone, and the letter was never put in. Let me pass over, my darling *sister*, the awful horrors which succeeded. ... After the laudanum was rejected from the stomach, I became calm, and to a casual observer, sane, so that I was suffered to go back to Providence.

Laudanum is opium dissolved in alcohol, and Poe had taken a heavy overdose not only of the strong narcotic but of alcohol as well. The two poisons were too much for him, and, as he says, his stomach rejected the mixture.

In this same letter, he went on to say that he had seen Mrs. Whitman while in Providence but that it was Annie he really loved. He asked nothing of her but to be allowed to take a small cottage at Westford, a small town a few miles west of Lowell, and live there with Mrs. Clemm as his housekeeper, in order to be near his beloved Annie.

He still believed that he was also in love with Mrs. Whitman and wrote to her a week later to acknowledge a note she had sent to him. After telling her that he was now completely recovered, he added: "*Still* the Shadow of Evil haunts me, and, although I am tranquil, I am unhappy. I dread the Future—and you alone can reassure me."

He wrote to her again two days later to warn her about the women who were maligning him, particularly Mrs. Ellet. In one of his letters he said, "Would it *not* be 'glorious,' *darling*, to establish, in America, the sole unquestionable aristocracy—that of intellect—to secure its supremacy—to lead and control it? All this I *can* do, Helen, and will—if you bid me—and aid me."

He was counting on marrying Mrs. Whitman, and she, on her part, evidently expected to marry him. Her mother was strongly opposed to the match, and, in order to protect her daughter's estate, had legal papers drawn up which transferred all her property to the mother. One of these had to be signed by Poe so that his agreement to the transfer would be on record. The documents were mailed to him in Fordham for his signature.

He may have taken them with him when he went to Providence to lecture on December 20. By this time, his ardor had cooled, for on the day he left New York he said, "I am not going to Providence to be married, I am going there to deliver a lecture on poetry." Then he added, "That marriage may never take place."

It never did, although not because of any reluctance on Poe's part. He lectured to a large audience and afterward had some drinks with a few of its members. On Friday, December 22, he signed the papers consenting to the transfer of Mrs. Whitman's property to her mother. The next day he wrote to the local minister asking him to publish the banns of matrimony. The marriage was to take place on Monday, and the newly wedded couple were to go to Fordham on Tuesday.

Poe and Mrs. Whitman spent most of Saturday preparing for the move. During the afternoon, an anonymous note was delivered to Mrs. Whitman which cautioned her against an imprudent marriage and made several charges against Poe which she had not heard before. Worst of all was an account of the way he had been drinking in Providence not only on the night after the lecture but that very morning. And this after he had solemnly promised never to touch liquor again!

The news gave Mrs. Whitman the excuse she had perhaps been looking for. She countermanded the order for the marriage banns and told Poe that she had done so. Then followed a scene in the best traditions of Victorian melodrama.

She listened to Poe's explanations with the "marble stillness of despair." But there was nothing silent about her mother, whom Poe called "an old devil." She became so furious at Poe that her daughter soaked a handkerchief in ether and inhaled that powerful soporific until she became unconscious.

Poe decided to give up the struggle and left the house muttering about the "intolerable insults" he had received there. He never saw Mrs. Whitman again.

In a letter that Poe wrote to Annie Richmond a few weeks later, he said: "From this day forth I shun the pestilential society of literary women. They are a heartless, unnatural, venomous, dishonorable set, with no guiding principle but inordinate self-esteem." But, as so often happened with Poe, he did not keep his promise to himself. In fact, he found out that he could make much-needed money by acting as an adviser, an editor, and a promoter to literary women who had the means to pay for the services of a distinguished literary man.

He wanted money now, he said. In this same letter he told Annie, "I must get rich—rich. Then all will go well—but *until* then I must submit to being abused." And he also said, "To be poor is to be a villain."

Apparently Annie's meek and mild husband was finally disturbed by the rumors he was hearing about the noted man who was paying such open attention to his wife, for Poe told Annie, "I deeply regret that Mr. R——— should think ill of me. If you can, disabuse him—and at all times act for me as you think best."

Perhaps it was Poe's sudden desire to become rich that induced him to start working hard again. It was at this time that he wrote "Hop-Frog," his most horrifying tale of revenge.

Although Poe had often complained about the hardships of being an author, he now put himself on record when he wrote to F. W. Thomas, a novelist he had known since 1840:

> Literature is the most noble of professions. In fact, it is about the only one fit for a man. For my own part, there is no seducing me from the path. I shall be a *litterateur*, at least, all my life; nor would I abandon the hopes which still lead me on for all the gold in California. Talking of gold, and of the temptations held out to "poor devil authors," did it ever strike you that all which is really valuable to a man of letters —to a poet in especial—is absolutely unpurchaseable? Love, fame, the dominion of the intellect, the consciousness of power, the thrilling sense of beauty, the free air of Heaven, exercise of body and mind, with the physical and moral health which result—these and such as these are really all that a poet cares for.

He could change his mind quickly, for this statement was made less than a month after he had said that he had to get rich.

He was making a rapid recovery from the emotional crisis —and humiliation—that his involvement with Mrs. Whitman had brought upon him. He felt that living in Fordham had broken his contacts with the literary world. "Living buried in the country makes a man savage—wolfish. I am just in the humor for a fight. . . . I am in better health than I ever knew myself to be—full of energy and bent upon success."

He planned to give up the cottage in Fordham; then he suddenly renewed the lease for a year. He was sending out article after article to magazines and selling some of them, but the publishing business was in a bad way. In a letter to Mrs. Richmond, he summed up the state of the market:

> The Columbian Magazine . . . failed—then Post's Union (taking with it my principal dependence); then the Whig Review was forced to stop paying for contributions—then the Democratic. . . . and then [another magazine] (from which I had anticipated so much and with which I had made a regular engagement for $10 a week throughout the year) has written a circular to correspondents, pleading poverty and declining to receive any more articles. More than this, the Southern Literary Messenger, which owes me a good deal, cannot pay just yet, and, altogether, I am reduced to Sartain and Graham —both very precarious.

Probably as a result of all this disappointment and misfortune Poe became ill again and was having symptoms of heart trouble. Yet this was a productive period for him. During it, he wrote "For Annie," with its prophetic lines:

> And the fever called "Living"
> Is conquered at last.

The short poem "Eldorado" also deals with the imminence of death. But Poe was now writing other verse as well. He paid tribute to Mrs. Clemm in "To My Mother," for she was his substitute mother-figure. He then wrote what has been called one of the great lyric poems of the English language: "Annabel Lee." It was his last poem.

The prose he wrote during this period is not outstanding. "Landor's Cottage" has a description of Mrs. Richmond, and the cottage is an idealized model of the real one in Fordham. Actually, the tale is connected with an earlier story, "The Domain of Arnheim," in which the heir to a fortune of $450,000,000 builds for himself a walled-in Paradise that has every natural splendor the Victorian imagination could conceive of.

In "Mellonta Tauta," Poe, again making use of the device of a manuscript found in a bottle, visits the year 2848 to describe the crossing of the Atlantic in a balloon which had all modern conveniences for its numerous passengers. The world he describes is so overcrowded that the life of an individual no longer matters, and the giant tyrannical figure of Mob dominates the earth.

This fear that the masses might take over was not new to Poe. In his early poem "Tamerlane," he had used the word "rabble-men," and in 1845, when he wrote "Some Words with a Mummy," he had expressed his low opinion of democracy. In this piece he had said that the consolidation of states, by which he obviously meant American states, had resulted in "the most odious and insupportable despotism that was ever heard of upon the face of the Earth." And, he added, "the name of the usurping tyrant . . . was *Mob*."

There is no doubt that Poe shared the prejudices of the Southerners he had grown up with. This was particularly true of his attitude toward slavery. He never questioned its validity and believed that the enslaved blacks were intended to be servants.

During this last year of Poe's life, short prose pieces as well as verse came from his ever-busy pen. They are all inferior to his best work in that medium. One of them, "Von Kempelen and His Discovery," deals with making gold out of lead. It was written at a time when the discovery of gold in California was having a tremendous effect on American development. This semihoax was intended to cast doubt on the value of this precious metal as money.

Among the poems Poe wrote at this time is the short one entitled "A Dream Within a Dream." The idea for this goes back to 1827 and 1829, when he wrote "Imitation" and "Should My Early Life Seem." But the 1849 poem ends with the revealing lines:

> Is all that we see or seem
> But a dream within a dream?

13

Journey to the Beginning of Night

■◆◆■

Over the Mountains of the Moon,
Down the Valley of the Shadow
—"ELDORADO," 1848

Early in May 1849 it looked for a while as if Poe's lifelong
desire to have his own literary magazine might at last be
realized. He had had some correspondence with Edward H. N.
Patterson, a young newspaper publisher who lived in Oquawka,
Illinois, a small town on the banks of the Mississippi River.
Now he received a letter from Patterson asking for detailed
information. Poe was so taken by surprise that he delayed
sending a reply for a week so he could consider the matter.

The project had to succeed, he told Patterson, and explained that he shrank "from making any attempt which may
fail." One obstacle, however, was Oquawka. The very name
of the place was against it; so was its location. Perhaps they
could say on the title page: "Published simultaneously at New
York and St. Louis." Oquawka was 150 miles north of St.

Louis, but St. Louis at least was a city that people had heard of. A literary magazine would not be taken seriously if it issued from a little Midwestern town with an odd name.

He told Patterson that he would be in Boston and Lowell for a week and then go south to Richmond. He asked for an advance of $100 for travel expenses. The first half should be sent to him in Richmond in care of the editor of the *Southern Literary Messenger*.

Patterson dutifully sent the $50, but Poe was delayed in starting out. He wrote to the *Messenger*, asking the editor to forward the letter from Oquawka. While in Lowell, where he spent some time with Annie Richmond, he was so desperate for money that he drew a draft for $50 on *Graham's Magazine*, which he felt owed him at least that much for manuscripts they were holding for publication. The draft was quickly returned, putting Poe to great "annoyance and mortification."

He returned to Fordham and then left there at the end of June with Mrs. Clemm. They stayed in downtown Brooklyn with Mr. and Mrs. Lewis, with whom he had become friendly while acting as the poetess's critic, editor, and publicity agent. He started out on the side-wheel steamer that took passengers to South Amboy and appeared to be in good spirits when he bade farewell for the last time to Mrs. Clemm, who had accompanied him to the dock.

On the short voyage down the lower harbor, or perhaps on the train that slowly made its way across New Jersey to Camden, something happened to the brilliant mind that was beginning to disintegrate.

While on the train, Poe according to his own account,

became convinced that two men seated behind him were planning to kill him. They got off the train before it reached the end of the line, but he was still disturbed when he finally arrived in Philadelphia. He apparently spent the night in the home of a friend there and left the next day.

He reached Philadelphia on the evening of Friday, June 29, disappeared the following morning, and was not seen again until Monday. What happened during that lost week end is not known except for Poe's vague ramblings about it. Late Monday afternoon he called at the house of John Sartain, whom Poe knew well. Sartain said that his visitor was in a sad state and was still frightened by the thought of the two men on the train. Poe asked his host to trim off his mustache so he would be less recognizable. Then he became restless and wanted to go out to see the Schuylkill River, although night was falling. Sartain lent him a pair of slippers to replace his badly worn shoes.

They went together on foot and by omnibus to the Fairmont Bridge, where they ascended a long flight of wooden stairs that led to the top of a nearby reservoir. They sat down on seats built on the first landing, and there Poe told Sartain that he had been arrested and confined in Philadelphia's Moyamensing Prison, where a beautiful young woman had appeared on the top of a high stone tower. They talked to each other from afar. He said that she had shown him some of the torments he would have to undergo:

> Great caldrons of boiling liquor, steaming and fizzling in the moonlight. But I saw the trap set by the conspirators, and told her so, boldly. If I once faltered, down, down, she would plunge me to the chin in the burning brandy, there to

squirm . . . with parched throat, burning eyeballs, and agonies of pain. Then a pack of demons brought my mother [Mrs. Clemm] to the caldron, chopped off her feet before my eyes, then her knees, her thighs, her arms, and at last plunged the poor, bleeding trunk into the reeking, bubbling caldron.

A few days later, when he told another friend about his supposed imprisonment, he said that in his dream he had flown over the rooftops of Philadelphia and had become a huge, black, evil-looking bird (a raven?) which told him that it was the embodiment of cholera, a disease that was then prevalent in the city.

When Sartain asked Poe why he had been sent to prison, he said that he had been accused of trying to pass a $50 counterfeit note. (The draft he had drawn on Graham's Magazine a few weeks before?) But Sartain, writing later about Poe's brief visit, said that he had probably had "a drop too much." Records of the prison do not list Poe's name or any of the pseudonyms he is known to have used.

He remained in Philadelphia for several weeks, although it is not known where he stayed. On July 7 he wrote a rather incoherent letter to Mrs. Clemm:

> I have been so ill—have had the cholera, or spasms quite as bad, and can now hardly hold the pen.
> The very instant you get this, come to me. The joy of seeing you will almost compensate for our sorrows. We can but die together. It is no use to reason with me now; I must die. I have no desire to live since I have done "Eureka." I could accomplish nothing more. For your sake it would be sweet to live, but we must die together. You have been all in all to me, darling, ever beloved mother, and dearest, truest friend.

I was never *really* insane, except on occasions where my heart was touched.

I have been taken to prison once since I came here for getting drunk; but *then* I was not. It was about Virginia.

Poe was evidently quite ill at this time as his next letter to Mrs. Clemm indicates. He had remained in Philadelphia until July 13 and then gone to Richmond, where he wrote this account of what had happened in Philadelphia.

Oh, Mother, I am *so* ill while I write—but I resolved that come what would, I would not sleep again without easing your dear heart as far as I could.

My valise was lost for ten days. At last I found it at the depot in Philadelphia, but (you will scarcely credit it) they had opened it and stolen *both lectures*. Oh, Mother, think of the blow to me this evening, when on examining the valise, these lectures were gone. All my object here is over unless I can recover them or re-write one of them. . . .

I got here with two dollars over—of which I inclose you one. Oh God, my Mother, shall we ever again meet? If possible, oh COME! My clothes are so *horrible*, and I am so *ill*, Oh, if you *could* come to me, *my mother*. Write instantly— oh *do* not fail. God forever bless you.

Five days later he again wrote to Mrs. Clemm, revealing the fact that he had been suffering for the first time from delirium tremens (*mania-à-potu*), the terrible hallucinatory disease caused by excessive drinking.

Most of my suffering arose from that terrible idea which I could not get rid of—the idea that you were dead. For more than ten days I was totally deranged, although I was not drinking one drop; and during this interval I imagined the most horrible calamities. . . .

All was hallucination, arising from an attack which I had never before experienced—an attack of *mania-à-potu*. May Heaven grant that it prove a warning to me for the rest of my days. If so, I shall not regret even the horrible unspeakable torments I have endured.

Once he was in Richmond, the city of his youth, Poe seems to have recovered his health. He stayed at the Swan Tavern, a fairly good hotel near the center of town.

A young Richmond woman, whose poetry had been praised by Poe, was greatly impressed by him, and noted that he seemed to be "a refined, high-bred, and chivalrous gentleman." He radiated "indescribable charm," she said, "almost magnetism, which his eyes possessed above any others that I have ever seen."

One might think that the dreadful attack of delirium tremens in Philadelphia would act as a deterrent, but it did not. Poe began drinking again, and this time he became so ill that a doctor told him that further indulgence would surely kill him. He joined the Sons of Temperance and took the pledge not to touch liquor. But in Richmond any meeting with friends called for the serving of some kind of alcoholic beverage, so the pledge was soon broken.

Poe was well enough to give three lectures on "The Poetic Principle" and read "Ulalume" at Old Point Comfort. He did very little writing but kept busy trying to promote his projected magazine. During the summer he wrote to Patterson, who had been trying to persuade him to reduce the yearly subscription price from $5 to $3. "The mere idea of a '$3 Magazine' would suggest namby-pamby-ism and frivolity," he said, and it would surely fail because he could not undertake it "*con amore*" (with love). He was still too feeble to travel, he added, but he hoped to be able soon to go to St. Louis to meet Patterson.

But something was now taking place which looked as if it might solve all the financial problems of Poe's life. He again met Sarah Elmira Royster, the girl he had been in love with twenty-three years before, when he was a student at the University of Virginia. Alexander B. Shelton, the man her father had induced her to marry, had died in 1844, leaving her an estate of $50,000.

Marriage to this wealthy widow now became the dominant interest in Poe's life. He went to her home one Sunday morning when she was about to go to church. Nothing could interfere with that, but she invited him to call again. He did so and promptly proposed to her. She hesitated and said later that they had never really been engaged but admitted that there had been "a partial understanding" between them, although on her part there were many serious doubts.

But there were no doubts in Poe's mind, although it would be unfair to charge that it was only Mrs. Shelton's money that motivated him. He remembered her well from the days of their youthful love affair; she was still attractive, and he knew from long experience that he needed a woman to take care of him. In fact, he evidently needed more than one woman as a letter written in August to Mrs. Clemm clearly shows: "Elmira talks about visiting Fordham—but I do not know whether that would do. I think, perhaps it would be best for you to give up everything there and come on here. . . . Could we be happier in Richmond or Lowell?—for I suppose we could never be happy at Fordham—and, Muddy, I must be somewhere where I can see Annie." After saying again that he wanted to live near Annie, he asked Mrs. Clemm not to tell him anything about her "unless you can tell me that Mr. R. [her husband] is dead."

It was evident that he thought the marriage to Mrs. Shelton would soon take place, for he said that he already had the wedding ring and was quite sure he would have no difficulty in getting a dress coat.

He still thought so on September 18 when he wrote to Mrs. Clemm again. He assured her that Mrs. Shelton loved him devotedly and that he could not help loving her, but nothing was yet settled. His most recent lecture had earned enough money for him to pay his hotel bill and have $2 left over. In a week he was going to Philadelphia to "revise" the poems of a lady whose husband was giving him $100 for the work. Then he would go on to New York and stay in Mrs. Lewis' home in Brooklyn. He thought it better not to go to Fordham, he said mysteriously. Perhaps he was still afraid of the two men he had seen on the train coming from New York, for he told Mrs. Clemm to write to him in Philadelphia but not to sign any name and address the letter to E. S. T. Grey, Esquire. This was the pseudonym he had used when he wrote to Mrs. Whitman in Providence during the previous September.

"If possible I will get married before I start," he added, "but there is no telling. . . . I hope that our troubles are nearly over." His were, for this, and a short letter he sent to Mrs. Lewis that same day, were the last he ever wrote.

14

Deep into That Darkness

■◆◆◆■

And the fever called "Living"
Is conquered at last.
—"For Annie," 1849

The night before Poe left Richmond to return to New York he went to a party where he told his hosts that he had asked Rufus Griswold to act as his literary executor and showed them a reply in which Griswold agreed to do so. Poe was the last guest to leave, and as he turned to go, a brilliant meteor dropped down from the sky, leaving a trail of fire in its wake.

The next day he called on Mrs. Shelton, who later told Mrs. Clemm that he seemed very sad and complained of being quite ill. She felt his pulse and also thought he had a fever. She told him that he was in no condition to travel, but he bade her farewell and left.

During the evening he visited his friend, Dr. John Carter, and read the newspapers in his office. Then he mistakenly took the doctor's malacca sword-cane instead of his own walking stick. He stopped at Sadler's Restaurant to get something to eat and there met some men he knew.

Afterwards, those who had seen him there were strangely silent about what had happened that night. But the group did not break up until late, and then several of them had to help Poe get to Rockett's Landing, where the boat for Baltimore sailed at 5:30 A.M. on Thursday, September 27.

The boat arrived in Norfolk shortly after noon. Passengers who wanted to go to Baltimore had to change there to a steam packet which arrived at their destination at seven o'clock the next morning. Whether Poe got on the second boat or not is unknown. There are stories that he had gone to Philadelphia, where he had an appointment to help a poetess with her work, but he did not call on her.

Five days and nights passed during a period that was a blank to Poe. Then he came back to the world again like a fallen angel that had been rejected by Hell. On October 3, Dr. J. E. Snodgrass, a friend of Poe's, was handed this note:

> Baltimore City, Oct. 3, 1849
>
> There is a gentleman, rather the worse for wear, at Ryan's 4th ward polls, who goes under the cognomen of Edgar A. Poe, and who appears in great distress, and says he is acquainted with you, and I assure you he is in need of immediate assistance.

The fact that the semiconscious man was near a voting place gave rise to rumors that Poe had been made drunk and then used while in that condition as a "repeater" at the polls, but there is no proof of this.

Dr. Snodgrass said that he found Poe in a barroom

sitting in an armchair with his head dropped forward. . . . His face was haggard, not to say bloated and unwashed, his hair unkempt, and his whole physique repulsive. His forehead was shaded from view by a rusty, almost brimless, tattered and ribbonless palm leaf hat. His clothing consisted of a sack coat of thin and sleazy black alpaca, ripped more or less at several of its seams, and faded and soiled, and pants of a steel-mixed pattern of cassinette, half-worn and badly fitting. . . . He wore neither vest nor neckcloth, while the bosom of his shirt was both crumpled and badly soiled. On his feet were boots of coarse material, and giving no signs of having been blackened for a long time.

The doctor wrote this account eighteen years later, so some of its details may be incorrect, but there can be no doubt of its essential accuracy. The clothes Poe was wearing were not those he had left Richmond in, so someone must have stolen them and substituted inferior ones. Strangely enough, he was still clutching Dr. Carter's sword-cane. This was an article of some value, the sort that thieves would not ordinarily have overlooked.

A carriage was summoned to take the semiconscious man to the Washington College Hospital. There he was placed in charge of Dr. J. J. Moran.

Five weeks later, the young doctor wrote to Mrs. Clemm to describe what had happened at the hospital. Poe had remained unconscious until three o'clock in the morning, when he awoke and shuddered violently. He began to talk with "spectral and imaginary beings on the walls. His face was pale and his whole person drenched in perspiration." He rambled on, and it was hours before he became quiet.

Dr. Moran left word that he was to be called when his patient became conscious again. He then questioned the enfeebled man but got only incoherent and unsatisfactory answers. At one time Poe told him that he had a wife in Richmond, so his mind evidently was going back into the past. Moran was unable to find out anything about the recent trip with its missing days. The doctor tried to encourage him by saying that he would soon be well enough to enjoy the company of his friends, who would surely come to the hospital to visit him. At this, Poe was suddenly roused to a burst of energy and said that "the best thing his best friend could do was to blow out his brains with a pistol." After that he was quiet for a while, then he became delirious again and was so violent that two husky attendants had to hold him down in bed.

Periods of delirium and unconsciousness alternated until Saturday night when he began calling out the name "Reynolds." The work of Jeremiah N. Reynolds was one of the sources Poe had used in 1837 when he wrote *The Narrative of Arthur Gordon Pym*. Yet it may be that the Reynolds he was summoning was someone else—perhaps a person with that name whom he had encountered on his nightmare journey from Richmond to Baltimore. One of the three election judges at Ryan's Fourth Ward Polls—near the barroom where Poe was found—was named Henry R. Reynolds. Poe may have appealed to this judge for help during that already forgotten period.

He kept calling the name Reynolds until three o'clock in the morning of Sunday, October 7. By that time he was so exhausted that he again became unconscious. At five o'clock he awoke, moved his head, and said quietly: "Lord help my poor soul." With that, Edgar Allan Poe, poet, writer of fantasy fiction, inventor of the detective story, journalist, editor, critic, and author of many articles, achieved the death he had so often longed for.

It was raining when they buried him in the Baltimore Presbyterian Cemetery at Fayette and Green Streets. Only four people, men who hardly knew him, came to the funeral, and the brief ceremony was quickly over.

Word of Poe's death had gone out by telegraph, and some—but by no means all—city newspapers printed a short account of his death. Most of them were favorable as obituary notices ordinarily are. But the misfortune that had plagued Poe all his life was still at work. The man he had appointed to be his literary executor, the Reverend Rufus W. Griswold, wrote a long article for the *New York Tribune* of October 9, which was the first of several efforts he made to damage the reputation of the writer whose estate he was supposed to protect and administer.

"Edgar Allan Poe is dead . . . ," he wrote. "This announcement will startle many, but few will be grieved by it. . . . He had few or no friends. . . . His harsh experience had deprived him of all faith in man or woman." Then he quoted a long description of Francis Vivian, a character in Bulwer-Lytton's *The Caxtons.* Vivian was an arrogant, irascible, envious, and ambitious young man who, Griswold said, was very much like Poe. Griswold did not sign his own name to the article but used the pseudonym "Ludwig." This malicious article was widely reprinted and was published even in Richmond, where the *Enquirer* gave it space.

Fortunately, Griswold's attack was not allowed to go unchallenged. N. P. Willis wrote a long and highly favorable account of Poe for the *Home Journal*, saying that there was much goodness in the man who had just died; Henry B. Hirst also praised him in the *Model American Courier*. He had known Poe during his Philadelphia years and said that he had always found him to be hospitable, gentle, and gifted as a writer but "unfortunate in every sense of the word." Lambert Wilmer, who had been acquainted with Poe since his *Southern Literary Messenger* days in Richmond, came to his defense and denounced the author of the obituary article as a "slanderous and malicious miscreant" who was afraid to sign his own name to the piece he had written. And John R. Thompson, editor of the *Messenger*, also praised Poe's work and said that "the mantle of forgetfulness" should be thrown over his infirmities. He quoted Longfellow as saying that Poe was "richly endowed with genius" and that the harshness of his criticisms was due to "the irritation of a sensitive nature, chafed by some indefinite sense of wrong." He was being very kind, for Poe had been unduly harsh with him.

But Griswold was not content with the mischief he had done in his "Ludwig" article. As Poe's literary executor he was in a position to profit from the rights to the prose and poetry that had come into his possession. A few days after Poe's death he persuaded Mrs. Clemm to give him all the manuscripts, published and unpublished, which she had and also to sign a document giving him power of attorney to act in her behalf. According to him, Mrs. Clemm was to have "all the profits that do not go to the booksellers," but even though Griswold said several times that he was not paid for his work, it seems unlikely that a man so avid for money as he was would have gone unrewarded. Mrs. Clemm died poor, and all she got from Poe's estate was the right to try to peddle some of his published books to friends.

Neilson Poe tried to put in a claim for the dead writer's retarded sister, Rosalie, but she apparently did not receive anything. Since Poe had sold the copyrights of some of his work outright, the estate was in doubtful condition anyway. But Griswold went right ahead, collecting enough material to fill four thick volumes. The first two of these were issued in January 1850; the third, which came out later in the year, contained Griswold's "Memoir," which was an expansion of his "Ludwig" article.

In this, he changed and even deliberately forged some of the passages in Poe's letters. In every instance, the dead writer came off worse from Griswold's alterations. He even invented incidents—or misrepresented what had actually happened— to cast a bad light on the man he was writing about. Few— if any—literary figures have been so maligned as Poe was by the editor he himself had appointed to keep his work before the public eye.

There is no doubt that Griswold was an odd creature. His own accounts of his behavior show that there was some-thing basically wrong with him. On one occasion, while cross-ing on the Brooklyn ferry with some important papers, he lost them by "falling from the boat in a fit." He was saved after he had gone down twice, but he was not grateful to his rescuers. He charged them with being "in too great a hurry . . . to row about for the floating letters or to dive after the pencil, knife, and small change that had escaped me."

Griswold was Poe's evil star; what he did hurt the dead

writer's reputation for years to come. The fourth volume of the collected works did not appear until 1856. Critics by then had been so influenced by what Griswold had said that the reviewer for *The North American Review* ended his long notice by saying that he wanted "some potent chemistry to blot out from our brain. . . . the greater part of what has been inscribed on it by the ghastly and charnel-hued pen of Edgar Allan Poe."

With such damning criticism as this, it was no wonder that Poe's reputation languished during the later part of the nineteenth century. He was by no means forgotten, but the four volumes of his writings, with Griswold's disparaging "Memoir" as a preface to the third, worked against the man who had been misfortune's luckless target.

15

The Poe Heritage

He was a goodly spirit—he who fell:
A wanderer by mossy-mantled well—
A gazer on the lights that shine above
A dreamer in the moonbeam by his love.

—"AL AARAAF," 1829

Edgar Allan Poe lived and died a poor man who had been badly paid for his editorial work and given only a pittance for his writings. Yet he left a large estate, an estate worth far more—then and now—than the property acquired by the men of wealth who were his contemporaries.

The editors who underpaid him are all forgotten; so are nearly all the journals that printed his work.

But the rich heritage that Poe left lives on, and the entire world shares in it, for his words have been translated into many languages. In 1845, while he was still alive, "The Purloined Letter" and "The Gold-Bug" were published in France. A year or two later, Charles Baudelaire, the poet who was to become famous as the author of Les Fleurs du Mal, discovered the American's work and was so moved by it that he began a series of translations that were to occupy him for years. Although Baudelaire was then young and unknown (*Les Fleurs du Mal*, his first book, did not appear until 1857), Poe's writings appealed to the French, particularly to the poets of the influential Parnassian and symbolist movements. These writers changed the course of French poetry during the last half of the nineteenth century. Not only Baudelaire but Mallarmé, Verlaine, and Rimbaud were among the many French poets who listened to the voice from America and were affected by it. "Dreams, somnambulism, madness, a sense of the mystical relationships between the senses and the phenomena of nature are the heritage left by the American poet to Baudelaire and those who felt his influence," the French critic Maurice Barrès once said.

Poe became an important factor in shaping French literature for nearly a century after the first volume of Baudelaire's translations was published in 1852. Yet in America, Poe was all too often thought of as a sensationalist, a writer of horror stories, and a dabbler in exotic subjects like ciphers, hypnosis, and automatons. He was interested in all these things, but he went beyond them to astronomy, philosophy, and the nature of the universe. Even more important, he was a truly creative person whose best work is very good indeed.

Griswold's malicious Memoir was to cast a dark shadow over American opinion of Poe for years to come. Emerson dismissed him contemptuously as "the jingle man," and Henry James said that admiration of his work was the sign of an immature mind.

An attempt to rehabilitate Poe's reputation was made in 1860 by Sarah Helen Whitman when she published *Edgar*

Poe and His Critics. She began her brief book by saying that Griswold's Memoir was filled with "perverted facts and baseless assumptions" and then went on to praise the dead author as a poet, a short-story writer, a critic, and a brilliant conversationalist.

Her charges against Griswold were true, but she did not have the necessary documents at hand to prove how utterly unscrupulous Poe's literary executor had been. This was not done until 1941, when Arthur Hobson Quinn, in his fine biography, placed letters side by side to show how Poe's text differed from what Griswold had printed. The changes, omissions, and actual forgeries then became apparent. In one case, Griswold was careless enough to refer to a Poe article which had not yet appeared when the original letter was written.

But the evil influence of Griswold lingered on, and, except in France, Poe continued to be neglected, although some of the French translations eventually aroused interest in Spain and South America.

Poe's first biographer was English. In 1874–1875, J. H. Ingram published a four-volume collection of Poe's work with a long biographical sketch. In 1880 he expanded this sketch into a two-volume biography, which was based on extensive correspondence with people who had known Poe.

In 1877, W. F. Gill issued the first American biography. It is short and unimportant, although it is interesting to note that both he and Ingram were strongly anti-Griswold.

George E. Woodberry, a descendant of an old New England family, wrote a short biography which appeared in 1885. His background made it difficult for him to like the Bohemian

Southerner, who stood for everything he abhorred, but he tried to be fair. He expanded the book into a two-volume work which was improved by more research. It was published in 1909, the hundredth anniversary of Poe's birth.

Before this, however, collected editions of the works, other than Griswold's, were brought out in the 1880's and 1890's. They were superseded in 1902 when J. A. Harrison's *The Complete Works of Edgar Allan Poe* was published in seventeen volumes. The title is a misnomer, for there has never been a truly complete edition. Nevertheless, the Harrison *Poe* is the best and most useful collection of the writings in existence and will remain so until all the volumes in the new Harvard University Press edition are available. The first one came out in 1969.

The Harrison *Poe* contains a two-volume biography written with care and understanding by the editor. It has the best account of the year that Poe spent at the University of Virginia.

One might think that in 1909, the centenary of Poe's birth, many books would have been published about him, but except for the revised edition of George E. Woodberry's 1885 biography, nothing of importance was issued. However, a number of magazine articles appeared.

During the following decade, perhaps because of the First World War, very little work was done on Poe. Once the war was over, a sudden renaissance of interest began, and in 1926 three useful books came out. One was Hervey Allen's two-volume *Israfel: The Life and Times of Edgar Allan Poe.* Since Allen, who is best known as the author of *Anthony*

Adverse, was primarily a novelist, his book has some of the characteristics of a work of fiction in its style and treatment. Nevertheless, Allen made use of much recently discovered material.

So did Mary E. Phillips in *Edgar Allan Poe: The Man*, which also appeared in 1926. Her two-volume work has many hitherto unpublished illustrations and some new information, but it is unscholarly and poorly organized.

The other important 1926 publication was Joseph Wood Krutch's *Edgar Allan Poe: A Study in Genius*, which is not a biography but an interpretation in the Freudian manner. This is not the only attempt that has been made to apply psychoanalytic techniques to the mind and personality of Poe. Dr. J. W. Robertson's *Edgar Allan Poe: A Psychopathic Study* had appeared in 1922, and Marie Bonaparte's *Edgar Poe: étude psychoanalytique* came out in Paris in 1933; an English translation of it followed in 1949.

Ever since the 1926 breakthrough, books and articles on Poe and his writings have been issued without letup. By now, Poe is one of the most written-about American authors. Generally speaking, modern critics think well of him, although some adverse comment still appears. Most of it is directed at Poe's long-known weaknesses—his sentimentality, his pretentiousness in using unnecessary foreign words, his show of erudition, his selection of nobly born characters who dwell in castles and palaces, his avoidance of down-to-earth, simple, American themes. But such criticisms apply only to his stories and poetry—not to his nonfiction. Unfortunately, few readers go beyond the better-known tales and poems. It is by those, primarily, that Poe will be judged.

Nearly a dozen memorable poems and perhaps half a dozen truly fine short stories must be credited to this man, whose life was lived under circumstances that did not encourage creative productivity. And Poe must be judged against the background of his time and place. He alone, of all the American writers of the first half of the nineteenth century, has become a world figure. In France, he outshines not only his contemporaries but all other American authors.

English language critics and writers, from George Moore, D. H. Lawrence, Vachel Lindsay, Hart Crane, and T. S. Eliot to Edmund Wilson, have paid tribute to Poe as a creative artist. There are dissenters to be sure, but they are relatively few, although Ernest Hemingway and Aldous Huxley must be counted among them. Yet no writers, not even the world's greatest, are without their detractors. Compared to most, Poe has stood up well.

He certainly does not lack readers, especially among young people. A knowledge of the best of Poe's work is an essential part of one's education.

Material from Poe has been used in motion pictures and television. Almost without exception, his stories have been handled badly on the screen, although some of them could be made into truly fine pictures. Meanwhile, they still await writers, directors, and producers with enough imagination and innovative skill to treat them as the serious psychological studies that they are.

Poe, of course, is a psychoanalyst's dream; in his life and works one can find almost anything a Freudian wants to look for. In personality and ideas he has more in common with the French symbolists, Baudelaire, Verlaine, Mallarmé, Rimbaud, and other *poètes maudits*, than he has with most nineteenth-century American authors, yet he does present certain aspects in American life—its darker side, a side that is just as real as the more obvious extroverted and forever cheerful face that some Americans seem to think they must put on.

Although Poe was dedicated to night, terror, and the grave, he sometimes donned a mask, a mask of ridicule and forced humor. Even his face, with its two very different sides, symbolized his duality. He was the chronicler of death and destruction, but he also celebrated the tenderness of love and endlessly sought affection for himself. He was the hero of his own tales of troubled conscience.

Walt Whitman said of him:

> In a dream I once had, I saw a vessel on the sea, at midnight, in a storm . . . flying uncontrol'd torn sails and broken spars through the wild sleet and winds and waves of night. On the deck was a slender, slight, beautiful figure, a dim man, apparently enjoying all the terror, the murk, and the dislocation of which he was the center and the victim. That figure of my lurid dream might stand for Edgar Poe, his spirit, his fortunes, and his poems—themselves all lurid dreams.

And it is in that realm, of course, that Poe reigns supreme. He is a dark messenger from the still unexplored land where dreams originate and irrational images cross forbidden borders to enter our conscious thoughts. His tales are timeless; his poems are echoes from a forgotten world; his characters are not people but embodiments of death, pestilence, revenge, and sheer hatred, while his women are always on the edge of death. His world is narrow; his time span, short; and his settings, unreal. Yet within these limitations, he works his magic, which conquers logic and refutes reason. Once we have fallen under his spell, everyday surroundings drop away, and the ancient sorceries take over. Poe becomes the master of dark ceremonies, and his strangely caparisoned puppets enact the rites that celebrate the passage from what is to what is not.

Chronology

1809. Edgar Poe is born in Boston, Mass., on January 19.

1811. His mother, Elizabeth Arnold Hopkins Poe, dies in Richmond, Va., on December 8. Mr. and Mrs. John Allan take him into their home.

1815–1817. The Allans sail for England on June 22, and Poe goes to a London school from 1816 to 1817.

1818–1820. He goes to a boarding school in Stoke Newington, north of London.

1820. The Allans bring him back to Virginia and arrive in Richmond on August 2.

1821–1825. Poe attends several schools in Richmond and does well in them.

1825. Allan inherits his uncle's fortune. Poe falls in love with Sarah Elmira Royster.

1826. He enters the University of Virginia on February 14 and runs up gambling debts there, which Allan refuses to pay. Classes end in December. Poe returns to Richmond, where he finds that Sarah Elmira Royster's father has intercepted his letters and that she is engaged to Alexander B. Shelton.

1827. Poe quarrels with Allan and leaves Richmond on March 24 to go to Boston. While there, he enlists in the Army. *Tamerlane and Other Poems* is published. In the autumn, his battery is transferred to Fort Moultrie, near Charleston, S.C.

1828. In December, the battery is again transferred to Fortress Monroe, Hampton Roads, Va.

1829. On January 1, Poe is promoted to sergeant major. On February 28, his foster mother, Frances Allan, dies in Richmond. On April 15, he is discharged from the Army and returns to Richmond. He goes to Washington to seek an appointment to West Point. Stays in Baltimore with or near Mrs. Maria Clemm, his aunt. *Al Aaraaf, Tamerlane, and Minor Poems* is published in December.

1830. He returns to Richmond in the early spring. His appointment to West Point finally comes through, and he goes to the Academy late in June.

1831. He is court-martialed on January 27 and then expelled. He goes to New York on February 19, where *Poems by Edgar A. Poe* is published. He becomes ill, tries unsuccessfully to enlist in the Polish Army, and early in May, goes to Baltimore, where he lives in Mrs. Clemm's house. His brother dies there on August 1.

1832. The *Philadelphia Saturday Courier* publishes five of Poe's tales.

1833. He has now written eleven stories. One—"MS. Found in a Bottle"—wins the first prize of $50 in the *Baltimore Saturday Visiter* contest. He also sells a story to *Godey's Lady's Book*.

1834. On March 27, John Allan dies and leaves nothing to Poe.

1835. The *Southern Literary Messenger* publishes four of Poe's stories. In August, he goes to Richmond to work for the paper. Mrs. Clemm and Virginia join him there in October.

1836. On May 16, he marries Virginia, who is not yet fourteen years old.

1837. In January, he leaves the *Messenger*. In February, he and his family move to New York.

1838. In the summer, the Poes move to Philadelphia. *The Narrative of Arthur Gordon Pym* is published in July. "Ligeia" is published in September.

1839. In the spring, Poe is paid $50 for his work on *The Conchologist's First Book*. In May, he becomes co-editor of *Burton's Gentleman's Magazine*. In September, *Burton's* publishes "The Fall of the House of Usher," and in October, "William Wilson." In December, *Tales of the Grotesque and Arabesque* is published, although dated 1840.

1840. He leaves *Burton's* and plans to issue the *Penn Magazine*.

1841. In April, Poe becomes editor of *Graham's Magazine*. He meets Rufus W. Griswold. "The Murders in the Rue Morgue" and "A Descent into the Maelström" are published. He tries to get a Government job.

1842. In January, Virginia breaks a blood vessel while singing. Poe gives up editorship of *Graham's*. He meets Charles Dickens. "The Mystery of Marie Rogêt" and "The Pit and the Pendulum" are published.

1843. In January, "The Tell-Tale Heart," "The Black Cat," and "The Gold-Bug" are published. *The Prose Romances of Edgar A. Poe* is issued as a 12½ cent pamphlet.

1844. In April, the Poes move to New York. "The Balloon Hoax" and *Doings of Gotham* are published, also "The Purloined Letter."

1845. In January, "The Raven" is published. Poe becomes editor and then owner of the *Broadway Journal*. *Tales* and *The Raven and Other Poems* are issued as books.

1846. In January, the *Broadway Journal* ends publication. The

Poes move to Fordham. "The Cask of Amontillado" is published.

1847. On January 30, Virginia Poe dies. "Ulalume" is published in December.

1848. On February 3, Poe reads *Eureka* at the New York Society Library. It is published as a book in June. He lectures in Lowell, Mass., and meets Mrs. Nancy Richmond (Annie). In July, he goes to Richmond. On September 21, he meets Mrs. Sarah Helen Whitman in Providence, R.I., and proposes marriage to her. In November, he is again in Lowell, Providence, and Boston, where he tries to commit suicide. Late in December, again in Providence, he attempts to persuade Mrs. Whitman to marry him, but she refuses.

1849. E. H. N. Patterson, of Oquawka, Ill., is interested in financing a new magazine to be edited by Poe. On June 30, Poe leaves New York to go to Richmond to get subscribers for it. He breaks down on the way, visits John Sartain in Philadelphia, but is not able to start out again until July 13. In Richmond he sees his boyhood sweetheart, Sarah Elmira Royster, and plans to marry her. He gives several lectures. On September 27, he leaves Richmond for New York. On October 3, he turns up in Baltimore and is taken to the hospital, where he dies at 5 A.M. on October 7.

A Selected Bibliography

By Poe

(Dates represent first publication in book form. Books marked by an asterisk have been reprinted in facsimile. The date of the reissue is enclosed in parenthesis.)

*Tamerlane and Other Poems. By a Bostonian. Boston, 1827 (1941).

*El Aaraaf, Tamerlane, and Minor Poems. Baltimore, 1829 (1933).

*Poems by Edgar A. Poe. Second Edition. New York, 1831 (1936).

The Narrative of Arthur Gordon Pym. New York, 1838.

The Conchologist's First Book. Philadelphia, 1839.

Tales of the Grotesque and Arabesque. 2 vols. Philadelphia, 1840.

The Prose Romances of Edgar A. Poe. Philadelphia, 1843.

*The Raven and Other Poems. New York, 1845 (1942).

Tales. New York, 1845.

Eureka: a Prose Poem. New York, 1848.

The Works of the Late Edgar Allan Poe, with a Memoir by Rufus

Wilmot Griswold and Notices of His Life and Genius by Nathaniel Parker Willis and James Russell Lowell. 4 vols. New York, 1850–1856.

*The Complete Works of Edgar Allan Poe, edited by James A. Harrison, 17 vols., New York, 1902. This has been issued in a photographic reprint, but it is being superseded by the fine scholarly collected edition now being published by the Harvard University Press. The first volume, Poems, edited by Thomas Ollive Mabbott, appeared in 1969. Others will follow. Meanwhile, The Complete Poems and Stories of Edgar Allan Poe, edited by Arthur Hobson Quinn and Edward H. O'Neill, in two volumes, New York, 1946, has most of the material readers want.

The Letters of Edgar Allan Poe, edited by John Ward Ostrom, 2 volumes, Cambridge, Mass., 1948, has been re-issued with additional letters; New York, 1966.

These are all expensive books which are bought mostly by libraries. But the best of Poe's writings are available in paperbacks. Dwight Macdonald in his edition of Poems of Edgar Allan Poe, New York, 1965, recommends these:

"Three recent Poe anthologies, all cheap and good are: Philip Van Doren Stern's The Portable Poe (Viking), T. O. Mabbott's in the Modern Library (Random House), and the one in the American Century Series edited by Margaret Alterton and Hardin Craig (Hill & Wang). Stern has 54 pages of Poe's letters and the most literary criticism; Mabbott has the most poems and tales, also 23 pages of interestingly opinionated notes; Alterton-Craig has less Poe than the other two but makes up for it, or doesn't, by a formidable 'critical apparatus' —136 pages of introduction and 77 pages of notes. Adding R. P. Blackmur's New American Library paperback edition of The Fall of the House of Usher and Other

Tales, which includes *A. Gordon Pym* complete as well as an 'Afterword' by the editor that is short and masterful, one . . . can buy all the major writings, together with a great deal of scholarly data and comment, for less than $7." (Now a few cents more than $7.)

About Poe

Quinn, Arthur Hobson. *Edgar Allan Poe, a Critical Biography,* New York, 1941. Reprint, New York, 1969. This is by far the best and most reliable of all Poe biographies.

Allen, Hervey. *Israfel: The Life and Times of Edgar Allan Poe,* New York, 2 vols. 1926; 1 vol., 1934 (with corrections).

Bittner, William. *Poe, A Biography,* Boston, 1949.

Bonaparte, Marie. *Edgar Poe: étude psychoanalytique,* 2 vols. Paris, 1933; English translation, New York, 1949.

Fagin, N. B. *The Histrionic Mr. Poe,* Baltimore, 1949.

Gill, William F. *The Life of Edgar Allan Poe,* New York, 1877.

Ingram, John H. *Edgar Allan Poe: His Life, Letters, and Opinions,* 2 vols., London, 1880.

Phillips, Mary E. *Edgar Allan Poe: The Man,* 2 vols., Philadelphia, 1926.

Robertson, J. W. *Edgar Allan Poe: A Psychopathic Study,* New York, 1923.

Wagenknecht, Edward. *Edgar Allan Poe: The Man Behind the Legend,* New York, 1963.

Weiss, Susan Archer Talley. *The Home Life of Poe,* New York, 1907.

Whitman, Sarah Helen. *Edgar Poe and His Critics,* New York, 1860 (1949).

Winwar, Frances. *The Haunted Palace, A Life of Edgar Allan Poe*, New York, 1959.

Woodberry, George Edward. *The Life of Edgar Allan Poe, Personal and Literary*, 2 vols., Boston, 1909.

Criticism of Poe's Work

Cambiaire, Célestin P. *The Influence of Edgar Allan Poe in France*, New York, 1927.

Campbell, Killis. *The Mind of Poe*, Cambridge, Mass., 1932.

Carlson, Eric W. *The Recognition of Edgar A. Poe*, Ann Arbor, Mich. 1966.

Davidson, Edward H. *Poe, A Critical Study*, Cambridge, Mass., 1957.

Hoffman, Daniel. *Poe Poe Poe Poe Poe Poe Poe*, Garden City, N.Y., 1971.

Hough, Robert L. (edited by). *Literary Criticism of Edgar Allan Poe*, Lincoln, Neb., 1965.

Jacobs, Robert D. *Poe: Journalist and Critic*, Baton Rouge, La., 1969.

Moss, Sidney P. *Poe's Literary Battles*, Durham, N.C., 1963.

Quinn, Patrick. *The French Face of Edgar Allan Poe*, Carbondale, Pa., 1957.

Regan, Robert (edited by). *Poe: A Collection of Critical Essays*, Englewood Cliffs, N.J., 1967 (Twentieth-Century Views).

Index

About the Author

Philip Van Doren Stern is the author or editor of more than fifty books on subjects ranging from the Model T Ford to the Civil War and prehistory. Many of Mr. Stern's books deal with nineteenth-century American history and literature. He is the editor of *The Portable Poe* and *The Annotated Walden*, and the author of *Henry David Thoreau: Writer and Rebel*.

Mr. Stern was born in Wyalusing, Pennsylvania, and educated at Rutgers, which conferred on him the honorary degree of Doctor of Letters. He is a former Guggenheim fellow, and has worked in advertising and as a book designer. His interests, which are of course reflected in many of his books, include art, travel, and photography. Mr. Stern now lives and writes in Norwalk, Connecticut.